To Rose May,

I hope you find someth[...] that will help you in your own journey. Best wishes setting your own 3:59's!

God bless,

MY 3:59

D0678551

MY 3:59

THE MAN I AM CALLED TO BE

DAN KLEIN

Copyright © 2016 by Dan Klein

All rights reserved

Contents

PART 3: After the Rumble

PART 4: My 3:59

Introduction

On a windy morning in Oxford, England in 1954 something happened that would ripple through time and space. A lanky medical student who had finished a disappointing 4th, just off the podium in the Helsinki Olympics two year earlier, dug deeper and did the impossible. How easy it is in life when faced with a challenge or set back to just give up. But Bannister, rather than giving up, turned disappointment into triumph by becoming the first person to run a mile in less than four minutes.

Bannister's 3:59 mile was against all odds. Prior to him breaking the four minute mark it was accepted "scientific" fact that the human body was incapable of running a mile in under four minutes. It was thought that the human heart would explode or the Achilles tendon would rupture from the strain. Ignoring all of the naysayers Bannister set out to prove that it could indeed be done. And after breaking the record, and more significant the mindset, and achieving his 3:59 mile it took another runner just two months to break the unbreakable record. A decade later, a high schooler from Kansas accomplished the once unthinkable. Roger Bannister the runner went on to become Dr. Roger Bannister the neurologist. Neurologist study the brain and the spinal cord. What your mind tells your body is important.

Bannister's 3:59 provides for interesting sports trivia indeed. But bigger than that, it captures the spirit to a mindset and way of life. To have the courage to bounce back from a setback, to create the vision for your own 3:59, to work every day to move yourself closer to seeing that vision become a reality, and giving absolutely everything you have to reach the finish line.

There are goals. There are stretch goals. And then there are 3:59's. To overcome and bounce back from the setbacks and challenges we all face through life and to dig deep to achieve our own impossible. To give thought and purpose to our lives and create the vision of where we want to be, what we want to accomplish, what we have to overcome, and to break through the 4 minute barriers we all have. To pour everything you have and having given every ounce of effort you can give—and some you didn't know you had—to cross that finish line, that's when you receive the real prize: the realization that in life the limitations we have are largely self-imposed.

Life is not about what you can do but what can't you do. What we tell ourselves we can – or cannot do—is incredibly significant. Be it physical or our professional, personal, or spiritual aspects of life—or more likely all of them—approaching life with a 3:59 spirit is a life worth living. And, as I discovered as a husband and father of four young children, when life drops a bombshell like cancer on you on some random Monday morning the 3:59 spirit can be the difference between life and death.

That Day

I was standing in my kitchen just finishing the sandwich I threw together when my phone rang. It was Paul, my doctor, asking me if I had gotten the prescriptions filled.

"Hey Paul, I just dropped them off and was getting ready to go pick them up," I said.

It was January 13, 2014 and that day began like so many before. I kissed my wife Claire and daughter Natalie goodbye, dropped off our three boys at school, and stopped by the doctor to finally do something about the cough I had since Thanksgiving.

"Don't worry about the prescriptions. I need you to come back to the office."

"Ok, I can be there in 10 minutes."

Paul tells me to just come back to his nurse's station when I arrive back at his office and he'll be waiting for me. I hang up the phone and know something is wrong. We spent New Years with my brother Doug and his family at an indoor water park. Everybody there was coughing and hacking. He called earlier that week to say he had gone to see his doctor and has walking pneumonia. I don't even know what the heck that is. Paul is going to tell me I have some weird virus or something called walking pneumonia. That is the last thing I need right now.

It's a cold, gray and rainy day and I have a quick five minute drive to allow my mind to wander through all the possibilities.

I pull up to the office and take the elevator to the second floor. There's a line literally out the door almost to the elevator. It's flu season after all. I'm not a send-my-food-back-to-the-kitchen kind of guy unless there's a significant problem. So I just waited patiently in the back of the line. Partially out of respect to those in front of me but mostly because I really didn't want to find out what was waiting for me behind that door.

After about 90 seconds Paul's nurse pokes her head out the door, looks around the line long enough to make eye contact with me and says "Mr. Klein? Come on back."

Oh crap, this can't be good.

I have just enough time to be seated in the little room where I was just an hour before and in walks Paul. He sits down, opens up his laptop, rolls over on his stool, and begins to start talking to me as he turns the screen towards me and shows me my chest x-ray.

Now, I'm not sure what he was saying but I do know his tone was different. Softer. More friend than physician. More one father of young children to another. And while I didn't catch everything he said I caught the "C" word. Cancer.

I don't know what the playbook is when your world gets dumped on its head on some random Monday morning. I'm sure there are plenty of resources out there to help you when you find yourself here, in this moment. Had I known I would have prepared.

But therein lies the rub. A relatively fit, seemingly picture of health 40 year old man with 4 kids does not spend his idle time, if such time does exist, planning for how he should react to the news that he has cancer any more than he prepares for an asteroid hit or a nuclear attack.

"I'm sorry Paul. What are you saying?"

"I'm saying until we prove this isn't, this mass on your x-rays indicates you have cancer. And we need to….." and his words slip away.

I think of Claire. Claire is not with me. I think I was just told I have cancer. Do I cry? I don't feel like crying. Do I? Should I? Wait a minute, what did he say? In hindsight I feel cheated, not having Claire with me at that moment. My wife. My best friend. My partner in all things in life. She should have been allowed to be there at that moment so we could start this journey together. That's what Claire and I do best —we do "together." Raising kids, together. Going on trips, together. Our faith journey, together. Within the very first minute of my fight with cancer it has already landed its first of many low blows. It does not fight fair.

Paul is still talking but the words are meaningless. Something about lung cancer or something called lymphoma. I'm still digesting and holding it together pretty well when I notice—was that really?—a crack in his voice as he gently placed his hand on my shoulder and said "I'm sorry Dan…."

I'll never forget the next fifteen minutes. It was like watching a scene from a horror movie where it's so real that you feel like you're the character in the shot. When the scene ends you finally exhale not realizing you were holding your breath and darn happy to find yourself in a large comfy chair. Today, there's no pulling myself out of this shot.

Paul lays out the immediate action steps. We first have to figure out what that mass is. The radiologist report says it could be either lung cancer or lymphoma. Unlikely to be lung cancer since I don't smoke and, if by chance it is "Dan, we're in trouble."

Paul says his top 3 guesses are Lymphoma, Lymphoma, Lymphoma. That we can deal with, but we need to find out what it is and we just won't know for sure until we get a biopsy.

Thirty minutes ago I was debating between PB&J and a turkey sandwich. Now it's lung cancer or lymphoma. Paul motions for me to come with him to the nurse's station where he begins to quickly lay out the next steps and what we need to do and who we need to see. He's talking to me and putting something into his computer. He and his nurse both are quickly on the phone calling the different doctors' offices that I need to see.

The conversations go something like "Hi Jim, it's Paul. I've got a favor to ask. Any chance you can squeeze in someone for me tomorrow morning?"

I was granted this odd credential. This peculiar magic pass that I never thought of before and never knew existed. I later came to refer to it as the medical privilege card. At first, the medical privilege card is convenient. It is appreciated. But later you recognize it for what it is. Members of this club get moved to the front of the line. It means what you have is bad enough that doctors make others patients wait for you. Doctors come in early, stay late, or skip their lunch or tee time to see a member. Or, if you are in really bad shape, they cut a vacation short. You don't want the medical privilege card. It's a bad club. If membership came with an actual card, it'd be a heavy weight to bear in your wallet.

Of course, on this cold, rainy day in January, I'm not aware of all of that just yet. All I know is there's a mass in my chest and Claire isn't with me. I'm waiting at the busy nurse's station as Paul and his nurse are coordinating tests and doctor consults to get us in a position where we know what we're dealing with.

Several other nurses and techs are going about their business. Paul is calling someone and his head nurse is calling someone else to get this process started.

"Yes, a MRI scan in 30 minutes. I'll have him there."

"A biopsy Wednesday at 8:30? We need him to get into the pulmonologist on Tuesday then. Sure, I'll call him. Thanks."

After a couple of moments and the expressions on the faces of the other people around me I became eerily aware that they know. Everyone knows. Their looks of sympathy and compassion. The quick darting away of eyes to whatever was in front of them when I make eye contact with them. They know this guy was just told he had cancer and they are all thinking the same thing: "Poor guy. I'm sure glad it's not me."

Then my first benefit of privileges kicks in. "You're all set tomorrow for the pulmonologist and his nurse is hopefully going to get you in on Wednesday so he can do a biopsy." Then the second. "You need to go right now back to the X-Ray place. They'll be waiting for you to do a MRI scan." And finally "From there you need to go to the hospital and get lab work done. They will be waiting for you also." Privilege number three.

"Paul, will you call Claire?"

I know I can't tell her over the phone—literally. I don't think I could physically pronounce the words. I text her and ask her to call me. Hoping, but not hoping, she would call. What do I say? How do I tell my best friend I, we, have cancer? My wife and the mother of our four children?

She's working and I don't hear back from her and that's ok because I'm still digesting and processing. I walk out to the parking lot and get in my car to head back to the x-ray place. The world, my world, has stopped but, oddly enough, everyone else seems to still be in motion.

I make my way to the MRI imaging and I barely have time to text Claire again and tell her to call me because the privilege kicks in and they are indeed waiting for me before the door even gets the chance to close behind me. Thirty minutes later I'm at the hospital getting my labs done and text her again during my brief window thanks again to the privilege: "Mr. Klein? Come on back."

I've quickly ran the medical gauntlet thanks to the medical privilege card and find myself walking to my car to drive home. Absolutely stunned. I still can't call Claire. What do I say? Finally, as I pull in the driveway, I get a text from Claire. She has talked with Paul.

There are some moments in life that are just for you and the people you share that moment with. Moments that turn good teams into championship teams but that don't get outside the locker room. Things that old marines have never told their families but make those who shared fox holes in battle cling to each other and cry at their 50 year reunions. Things you just keep within the circle. You don't want to dilute or discount them.

Maybe it's being selfish. Maybe it's honoring and placing a premium on the moment and those involved. Maybe you know you just can't express it adequately enough with words so you just don't even try. Those moments in life when you are aware that this is a moment you will never forget and those you share it with will always have a common bond. A stronger bond.

Through these pages, I will bear a lot of my soul as I share my journey. And the perspective I have gained will hopefully help you and the people you love on personal journeys both big and small. But that moment, finally being together for the first time on that terrible day, that's our moment. Being with Claire for the first time after being told that cancer has invaded our home. That's just for us. In a culture of social media and posting seemingly everything, some things, the real things, are meant to be kept.

Chapter 1: Stepping On the Bus

Everyone has those moments. Some, I have come to learn, mark time for very difficult stretches. And some represent the best pivot points of life's journey.

For me, October 24, 1991 is one of those dates that is etched deep in my memory.

I was a freshman at Saint Louis University.

"There you are! Dan, get on the bus. We're having a date dash."

"Having a what?" I said to myself.

It was my first semester of college. I was coming back from making funnel cakes at a haunted house. The day's memory sits crystal clear in my head. Funnel cakes and haunted houses and I was hustling back to my dorm to call my girlfriend back home in Michigan.

The path to that very important phone call lead me past the corner of West Pine Blvd and Vandeventer Avenue. As I approached I saw a blue school bus filled with energy and people. As the last few people were stepping inside someone spotted me.

"No, sorry, I have some homework to do and got to get back."

My attempt at getting back to my room for my phone call was met with "Nope, you're getting on the bus right now." I reluctantly climbed onto the bus, grabbing the only seat available, right behind the driver. I hid my disappointment and put on a smile amidst the electricity that only 75 college coeds on a spontaneous outing can bring.

I came to learn that a date dash is when you're given thirty minutes to find a date. A half-hour to convince someone to go with you to an unknown destination and you need to get yourself and your date on the bus. So here I sit, as the big blue school bus pulled away from campus and into the city, date dashing without a date.

The bus took us to a little neighborhood bar. It's one of the more endearing qualities of St. Louis. Seemingly on every block in the older parts of the city, usually on the corner, you'll find a neighborhood bar. And that's where I met Claire.

Actually two Claires. Claire from Chicago and Claire from Kentucky. That's what I called them that night. They called me Dan from Michigan. It didn't take long before Claire from Kentucky became the focus of my attention. She was cute. She was sweet and kind. She had a small town charm along with that spark that some people just seem to have.

All the noise, the laughing and yelling and music, began to fade away. It became just us. Initially sitting alone in a booth talking and then eventually moving outside and sitting in the quiet of an adjacent alley. Beginning. With every newly learned fact about each other we started constructing our own world. Falling. Right there, that night. October 24, 1991. That world has been our wonderful place to live ever since.

For us, on that night, time stood still. So much so that the party had ended, everyone had been loaded on the bus, and had it not been for someone looking around the corner and seeing us, that bus would have pulled away without us.

At a neighborhood bar in the old part of St. Louis a monumental shift occurred in my life. A few hours before, I was rushing back to what, I thought, was the most important thing in my life. Stepping onto the bus was the last thing I wanted to do. I was not supposed to be there. How often our lives can change in a moment and when we least expect it. Those random dates in all of our lives that are so easy in hindsight to pluck from the years and decades gone by.

✳✳✳✳✳

In the last 25 years we've never really had an argument, let alone a fight. We had times, especially in that first year, where we'd have our heart-to-heart talks and would work through issues as our relationship evolved. But we've always communicated well. We've always respected each other. We hear people say marriage is hard work and marriage is difficult and marriage is a struggle. We just look at each other, smile, and shrug with a "seems pretty easy to us" kind of gesture.

At our church, we conduct premarital counseling for engaged couples. On one hand, we feel very qualified because of the richness and depth of our relationship. But on the other hand we feel very unqualified because it's not really something we had to work on. It just happened. And it's not much counsel for young couples to say, "It's easy. Be like us."

We dated for four years before I called Claire's parents, George & Gail, to ask them for her hand. They gave me the blessing I sought and the following week I asked Claire to marry me. After graduation we moved back to her small town home in Glasgow, Kentucky. Our plan was to move there for a year, pay off student loans, and then go see the world. We made it 35 miles down the road, to Bowling Green. Which has turned out to be the perfect setting to raise our family.

Life had been moving along nicely. Very nicely. Claire and I both had meaningful careers. We maintained our great friendships from our college years as well as from before. Twenty years after graduation I still get together with eight of my old college buddies annually. Many of those guys were on that big blue bus more than two decades ago.

After enjoying seven married years together as just us, traveling and doing whatever we wanted whenever we wanted, our family began to fill in. First John. Then Matthew and Ben—twins. And finally, little sister Natalie. Four kids in less than seven years. Busy.

Some days were easier than others. But every day was work. When you work together with someone towards a common purpose, be it as parents or teammates or business partners, you grow together. Every day presents a new day and with time we've come to appreciate that every stage of parenting has its own unique wonderful parts as well as its own unique challenges.

It was during that part of our life, the up-all-nights and countless pushes on the swing and drives in the van to finally lull someone to sleep, that I came to know one of my favorite qualities of Claire.

Claire has this uncanny ability to push through the toughest things. She's just able to put her head down and go to work. The really incredible part is that she makes it look *easy*. It's an amazing quality and has been a priceless asset to our family. Claire just has an extra gear of grace which helps make our home such a loving home.

In addition to that loving home we have great relationships with both of our extended families. Living so close to Claire's family they play a larger logistical role in our lives. But we see my family several times through the year despite the distance. We are blessed to have maintained old friendships while developing strong bonds with friends here in Bowling Green. Bonds that would grow only stronger through crisis.

Chapter 2: Ice Cream and Devotion

We have a tradition in our house of eating ice cream every night. At any given time we are known to have upwards of a dozen gallons of various ice cream flavors between the kitchen freezer and the deep freeze in the garage. The latter we bought primarily to store ice cream as Claire buys it in bulk when it goes on sale.

As our lives with kids began to get busier and we had ballgames and school events that cut into our family time we recognized we had to make the effort to take time for our family. It was important to us to carve out time on a regular basis. Time where we could just sit around the kitchen table and talk about the day and to end our day in prayer and gratitude. Time to remind ourselves that every day, even this horrible day, is a gift.

Not every night but on most nights the kids head upstairs to get ready for bed while Claire and I get the ice cream ready and try to put the house somewhat back together. And then we clear off the kitchen table. Remove it of all the clutter and distractions. Turn off all the lights except the one over the table. Light a candle as the kids make their way back downstairs to get their bowls of ice cream and come to the table.

And we sit there as a family and talk. Sometimes for ten minutes. Sometimes for 45 minutes. We just let the conversation about our everyday life occurrences move along trying to gently guide them, sometimes more successfully than others, to productive discussions about faith, values, and morals. Then we end with prayer.

We started using a book called *Jesus Calling*. There's a children's version and it works perfectly. It's a daily devotional with a title and a short bible passage along with 2-3 paragraphs of conversation as if Jesus was talking to you. We take turns reading it from night to night and afterwards everyone comments on what they thought it meant or maybe a certain passage or sentence that spoke to them.

The kids know to be respectful of someone else who is talking—although reminders are sometimes needed. They are also aware not to say "um" or "you know." Give thought to what you are going to say before you speak and express your thoughts clearly. We finish our time with saying something big or small that for that specific day we are thankful for. Usually "Mommy" is in there somewhere.

So on this most extraordinary day, just as many of the nights before, we set in motion our nightly routine. The kids are doing their usual thing and gathering around the kitchen table. Of course they have no idea what's going on. We don't really know what's going on. We just know ten hours earlier we were told there was a pretty good chance that mass on my X-ray was cancer.

Claire and I did our best at nonverbal communication. A look. A reassuring smile. A soft touch. A hug held a little tighter and longer than typical as we proceeded through that horrible day and into that night's devotion. A nonverbal dialogue we were already fluent in after 23 years together, but one we would master over the coming months. It would be a couple of weeks before we had the difficult conversation with the kids. We wanted them to continue to live in this innocent happy cancer-free world as long as they could.

Here we sat as we did many nights before. The kids are

busy doing their thing and the distractions and the busyness that four kids around a table eating ice cream brings. We, sitting opposite, just look at each other. Hurt. Scared. Loving. Masking it all with a little smile.

We gaze at each other across this special place. Around our kitchen table. Sacred ground in our family. The place in our home where a premium is purposefully placed. Not a catch all for clutter where only bits and pieces of surface see the light of day. A place that we clear every day. As if making a clean slate. So many nights before where we shared our days through laughter and prayer. Where we try to pass on our faith and family values in a subtle and consistent way. Where we end every day with what we are thankful for.

And Claire and I just look at each across the table. Not able to put our real emotions on display. Without discussing it we know immediately normalcy would be a priority. Despite this huge ugly invader into our family we know for the kids we need to keep things as normal as we could for as long as we can.

We began to transition the discussions around the table from ordinary things that day to our devotion. We opened by signing ourselves with the cross. As I begin the gesture I suddenly remembered from our couples' bible study a few years earlier as something soldiers would do before battle. A gesture my Grandma Hartman always did when she started her car before every trip. A simple and ancient way to welcome God into your space for guidance and protection.

I don't know how God does this. He seems to always put the right person, the right bible passage, the right whatever in our path at just the right time. It's His perfect timing. Beyond my understanding. As we opened up the *Jesus Calling* book I read the title for January 13th:

Expect Surprises!
This is the day the Lord has made; let us rejoice and be glad in it.

Try to see each day as an adventure, planned out by Me, your Guide. Instead of trying to make your day into what you want it to be, open your eyes to all the things I have prepared just for you. Each day is My precious gift to you—and you only have one chance to live it. Trust that I am with you every minute, working in your life. And then thank Me for this day no matter what happens.

Expect surprises! When you live your life with Me, no day will ever be boring or predictable. Don't take the easiest path. Don't just go through the day. Live it! Be willing to follow Me wherever I lead. Even when My way seems scary, the safest place to be is by my side.

Claire and I look at each other across that hallowed space and give each other sort of a relieved smile. As the kids begin their usual responses we know it's going to be a difficult road. But we trust. And we know wherever this road takes us we will be ok.

Chapter 3: Engine Turnover

About a year earlier, in early 2013, my Dad was diagnosed with gum and jaw cancer. That was a big jolt to our entire family. He had surgery at University of Michigan Cancer Center in Ann Arbor on April 16th. Dad, with his sense of humor and background as a CPA and accounting professor, half joked and half griped about the double whammy—tax day on April 15th and cancer surgery on April 16th. "Pow! The ultimate 1-2 punch" he quipped.

My brother Doug and sister Mary live in Grand Rapids, Michigan just miles from Mom and Dad. My sister Caroline lives in Chicago and my brother Don lives in Florida. Mom is from Mt Pleasant, Michigan which is about 2 hours north. Dad is from St. Louis, hence our connection to the city and a big reason I went there for college.

We all wanted to rally to support Dad and Mom. Having families of our own and busy lives we worked out somewhat of a schedule where we could make sure there was plenty of support there at all times. Both for the surgery and recovery.

He had major surgery. They cut off a good chunk of his jaw where the cancer was and took bone from his leg in an attempt to reconstruct the jaw. He had a trach to ensure breathing. His prognosis was fair but it would be a long, long road to recovery. A road he is still on today.

He was in ICU for several days before they moved him to a step down room. Although Dad was in his late 70's, you would never know it. I suppose between good genes and taking fairly good care of himself he was a pretty youthful guy. He'd say "just clean living".

Dad was a pretty good athlete in his day. He was the 77th pick in the 1958 NBA draft. He was also drafted by the Baltimore Orioles for baseball. With a little smile he would tell you how he figured there was more money in accounting back then.

Rockhurst College in Kansas City was where he displayed his athletic prowess. He was inducted into their Hall of Fame some years ago. It was the first time I think any of us were aware of his athletic accomplishments. Dad played college basketball in Kansas City the same time some guy named Wilt Chamberlain played up the road at Kansas. If you ask he'll tell you stories about how he would dribble around Wilt the Stilt much too fast for Wilt to contain him. Funny guy.

So as the surgery approached and the family began co-ordinating schedules I told Claire I wanted to be there for Dad. Of course. She understood, just as I would for her. Leaving our home for a day or two meant one person was left to do the heavy lifting of taking care of four kids. She'd call in her Mom, Gail, who was always there for us. I left early in the morning and would return home the next night in time for John's baseball game.

I got to Ann Arbor and found my way through the maze that is the University of Michigan's Cancer Center. Claire, a physical therapist, has that familiarity with hospitals. I, like most people, would prefer to stay out of hospitals as much as possible. The paint. The smells. The stories behind each curtain.

I made my way to Dad's room not sure what to expect. And there he was. The same guy who used to run circles around Wilt Chamberlain. The same guy who hit me countless ground-balls as a kid. The same guy who was always strong and right.

Struggling to do the simplest of task. They were trying to move him from the bed to his chair.

A male nurse and my sister Caroline were doing their best. My Mom, as usual, there for support and trying to do anything she can in that tiniest of space between a hospital bed and window. Obviously, in extreme discomfort, one side of his face swollen like a cantaloupe and tubes attached all over him.

He saw me and just cried. Sobbed. It was the first time I'd ever seen my Dad cry. So I cried. I went over and sat next to him. Not sure what I could or couldn't touch. He was a mess of IV lines, drainage tubes, and hospital garments. He couldn't talk but I'm not sure if he was aware of that and all that came out was some jumbled sounds.

Sometimes there's nothing to say. Sometimes life just dumps you in a spot where words are meaningless. You're just there. And that's all you need to be. There. You hold. You pray. You cry.

After a difficult couple of hours my sister Caroline, first born and protector, was well passed her designated shift and headed back to her family in Chicago with plans to return a few days later. Mary and Doug, who lived a couple of hours away, made the trip in after work and were heading back to their families. Like a lot of families these days the adult children who live closest to aging parents take on a disproportionate workload. I appreciate that and recognize the challenge of balancing your own family yet honoring your father and mother. That's not easy and takes a lot of grace from all people involved.

As the night wore on, Mom and I started the process of getting familiar with Dad's new routine. The steady stream of different doctors and nurses and eager to learn medical students. The different beeps and what they meant. The different tubes and lines. The most difficult thing was trying to communicate with Dad. He was still doped up which didn't help. He had a feeding tube down his throat which he tried, on more than one occasion, to yank out. And the poor guy was missing half his jaw. And, to beat it all, I don't think he realized we couldn't understand him.

If the situation wasn't so serious I could have enjoyed the comic value of it. Dad, in extreme discomfort, would blurt out something that sounded like an old engine trying to turn over. Totally unrecognizable. Mom and I would look at each other with a "You get that?" kind of look. Only to get the same look back from each other. Mom, hard of hearing, would lean in and politely say "What Sweetie?"

Out would come the engine turning over sound again. This time with a little mix of desperation and frustration.

Same look exchanged between us.

"Don, honey, I cant understand what you said. Did you want your pillow moved?"

Poor Dad's eyes would roll only that way that a married couple of 50 years, one a little hard of hearing and one with a little less patience than average, could. I enjoyed this scene for a brief moment until Dad, frustrated that Mom couldn't make sense of that ridiculous sound he was making, turned his desperate look to me.

Oh crap.

Engine turnover with eyes pleading "Surely son you know I'm what I'm saying??"

This time with a little added engine turnover and voice fluctuation, slowing down, and a little bit of hand gestures at the end as if explaining the original engine turnover.

Oh crap.

I have no idea what he's trying to say. So I do the best thing I can think of at the time.

"Pops, I'm going to get the nurse."

We labored through working out some hand signals

and eventually Dad had a marker and small wipe board next to him on the bed. The wipe board worked fairly well depending on where he was in his morphine cycle.

Right after a hit it was just scribble. To us anyways. To him it was perfectly clear. That was interesting.

Dad: Engine turnover. Scribble. Show us the board.

Mom and I: look at each other with that "You get that?" look only to get it returned.

Dad, eyes opening wide, with a look of amazement that we couldn't understand the engine turnover or for crying out loud the horrible scribble begins to tap the marker on the board while he turns over the engine again. Slowing down emphasizing certain points while now not so much as tapping the board but striking it.

Sorry Pops, we got nothing. More amazement from him. Rolling of eyes. Big exhale of frustration while we go to our last resort and most inefficient mode of communication. Randomly throwing out potential request in hopes of one landing close enough to its mark for him to stop shaking his head from side to side, his eyes closed in frustration, and get a quick and enthusiastic nod with eyes wide open. A grunt of relief as if to say "Yes, yes, yes. For crying out loud yes." Finally! His foot scratched, ice chips, pillow adjusted, or one of a hundred other possible things.

One of those was the bathroom. Getting Dad to the bathroom for the first time was a chore. It's amazing what we can take for granted. After lots of positioning of tubes and wires and walker, very slowly going from laying down to sitting, and plenty of engine turnovers we made it. We'd get him situated with the walker in front of him and coordinate all his drainage tubes with the rolling IV stand and its tubes. Trying to keep them all from getting tangled. I was better at it than Mom.

Something would get tangled up, which was very easy

to do, and regardless if I was responsible for that tube in our newly designed system or Mom was Dad gave her that "Oh Julie!" look. Then look at me and turn the engine over quietly as if to say under his breath "seriously, see what I've been dealing with for 50 years."

The doctors encouraged Dad to get up as often as he comfortably could. So that become his job. His number one objective. He knew that's what he could do to get him closer to getting the heck out of there and back in his own bed at home. That was the one and only part of the entire process he could control. And he made sure he did his part.

We made goals that every two hours we would get him up and walk. Funny how some things can be so hard to communicate but the important things are clear. After the doctor told Dad that was what he could do we went right to work. I used the "How's your pain today?" board that faced his bed as a chart. Down the left side I labeled out every two hours. Next to it a place for a checkmark. That was our mission.

We're not worrying about this entire incomprehensible rehab that would stretch years. We're just focusing on the part we can control. And, more specifically, only focusing on the very next part. What can I do right now? Do it and fill in the space with a check to for success. And that's exactly what we did.

The first time it was from the bed to the door. I wasn't sure we were going to make it. It took everything he had to cover the 20 feet to the door. But he made it. Check. Two hours later, as uncomfortable as it was, he wanted to get up. And did. The nurse's station was the goal. About fifteen feet past his door. Check.

Incidentally, on this trip I became officially in charge of absolutely all tubes and the IV stand. And, yes, the IV stand required to be unplugged every time. Otherwise the person connected to it, by a needle no less, got a very unpleasant surprise-when the slack runs out. "Oh Julie!" Engine turnover! Engine turnover!

When we made it to the nurses' station he was greeted with a "Well look who's out of bed?! Hello there sunshine!" the nurses said to Dad as we labored through the previous goal and another 15 feet to our next goal. Dad gave a little "Well what can I say ladies?" in engine turnover. I made a comment about the young ladies happy to see him and he delicately and slowly balanced himself on the walker with one hand and stroked his eye brow with the other. That's Dad signal for "I still got it".

He still had his sense of humor. That's a good sign. Over the next 12 hours the scene replayed itself. Each time the goal being a little farther. Stopping briefly at the nurse's station to charm. The painting on the wall another 20 feet down the hall. Check. The double doors past that. Check. Eventually we got all the way down the hall. Check. Dad was on a mission to do his part of the recovery. And he did it very well.

I wasn't aware of it at the time but Dad, as he always did, was preparing me. Preparing me for my own journey with cancer. A journey I never dreamed I'd be on.

There was another man on the floor that had the same surgery as Dad and was about 15 years younger. The doctors were aware of Dads age, 76, and the additional risk it imposed. But they reported to him how much better he was doing compared to the other guy. That only fueled Dad's drive. Sometimes encouragement is the perfect complement to prescription.

My time in Ann Arbor was coming to an end. My shift wrapping up. It had been a long 24 hours. A little bit of sleep here and there which probably did more harm than good. Doug was due to arrive later in the day. Mary just called to say she was almost there to tap in. Caroline and Don called to get the update and check in with Mom.

I was attempting to teach Mom how to text. We sent a message to Caroline and to Mary to give it a try. They responded promptly with impressed replies that Mom was texting. After the thread had a few messages I, then texting as Mom, sent them a message about how disappointed she was that her favorite child had to leave. They didn't bite on that one. We have this running friendly family debate about who is the favorite child. Mom and Dad of course do what Moms and Dads are supposed to do. So the debate continues.

I walked outside for some fresh air and to stretch my legs for the 500 mile trip ahead of me. I checked in with Claire and updated her and stopped by the cafeteria to grab a bite to eat and get a cup of coffee for the drive home. When I returned Mom was laying partially on the bed with Dad and partially on the recliner we had positioned next to the bed – out of the way of the IV cord. Leaning on each other. Both exhausted and both finally grabbing a bit of rest. On the wipe board at Dad's side, late enough in his morphine cycle for clarity of thought and handwriting, I made out his most recent scribble:

"We have wonderful children."

Chapter 4: Monday Night Call with Sean

It's 9:30 on Monday night. Ice cream is over and the kids are sleeping. It's been less than 12 hours since I first went to Paul's office. It's been the longest of days and the kids are thankfully oblivious to the gathering storm. Claire and are I exhausted. I get online and start Googling "lymphoma" and "Hodgkins" and "chemotherapy." Sometimes information can be helpful. Other times it can be overwhelming. After 10 minutes, at Claire's suggestion, I shut it off. It was the first and only time I did that.

I call Sean. Sean is the boy's inline hockey coach and a radiologist. He's also a husband and father of four children close to our kid's ages. I know him well enough to call him a friend but not well enough to call him at 9:30 at night.

"Sean, it's Dan. Sorry I'm calling so late. Do you have a few minutes?" Sean graciously takes my phone call and I proceed to tell him what I know.

He gives me the initial sympathetic apologies and offers whatever he can do to help. He says he can see if he can access the pictures. Sean works some from home and has the technical set up to do so. "Ok, yup, there it is. Can't be lung cancer. Could be thyoma or lymphoma. My guess is Paul is right that it's lymphoma."

Sean goes on to explain that there are two main classifications—Hodgkin's and non-Hodgkin's—lymphoma. Within each of those there are different sub-classifications.

"I'm 90% sure it's lymphoma but we won't know until a biopsy is done. Who is doing your biopsy tomorrow?"

I give him the name and he says "Great. He's a good doctor and a friend. I'll call him as soon as we get off the phone. Dan, this could be a non-cancerous tumor. Those happen. We just won't know until the biopsy."

Sean, along with Paul, becomes our inside man. More like our inside rock. Between Paul and Sean they provide the grease to allow the wheels of the machine that is medicine to turn smoothly for us through that difficult initial period. They are also in touch with us daily if not hourly. They have an update or if not at least a text to say "nothing yet".

It's irritating to me at times how much people are on their phones. Families go out to dinner and they are all in their own little individual world. In professional settings, people have their phones in their lap texting or posting. I would notice Sean on his phone when he was coaching. There he would be on the bench with his phone either in his hand or even up to his ear.

Really?? During a game??

For some people there are no legitimate excuse. I'm in that camp more times than I'd like to admit. But I won't judge that so quickly anymore. I now know sometimes on the other end of the line is a guy who has just found out he has cancer.

"This could be some rare virus and be nothing. A couple days in the hospital on meds and you're clear. That's not likely but it happens. I'm with Paul. My money is on lymphoma. If it is then we need to classify it between Hodgkins and Non-Hodgkins and then sub-classify it from there."

Sean walks us through every step and offers both his professional and personal opinion. I appreciate his honesty. In a world where we give every kid a trophy for just showing up and everyone is always winner despite ability or effort we run the risk of losing credibility. In an odd way it was nice to know Sean was giving it to me unfiltered and I could take his words at face value—good or bad. Waiting 24-48 hours for the phone to ring with your biopsy results is a very uncomfortable place to be. It's nice to at least know you're going to get a straight answer.

Chapter 5: Biopsies & Oncology

Prior to all this, I didn't know much about biopsies. I'm embarrassed to say I often got malignant and benign confused. I couldn't have told you what an oncologist was 24 hours earlier. But, like many things in life, when you experience it you know more details than you ever dreamed you could or would want to know.

It's 8:00 AM Tuesday morning and I pull into the hospital parking lot for the appointment with the pulmonologist. One of the favors Paul called in. Claire is dropping off the kids and then heading this way. Conveniently she works at the hospital and I'll text her when I get called back so she can join me. Like most people we're used to long waits at the doctor's office and there's no sense in both of us sitting there for who knows how long.

I step off the elevator at the 2nd floor and find the office number. It's inside the oncology department. I pause briefly before I approach the door with "Oncology" written above it. I'm eerily aware as I open the door and enter that I am crossing the threshold into a new world. The world of cancer.

I get checked in and grab a seat. It's a waiting room a little nicer than normal. There's a handful of other people there. I'm aware that I am significantly younger than everyone else. I barely get settled and sift through the magazines next to me when the door opens and the medical privilege kicks in.

"Mr. Klein?"

"Yes, Ma'am."

I follow her back and she takes me to an examining room. She begins to take my vitals and as she wraps up says the doctor will be with me shortly. I text Claire and let her know I'm back in a room but don't know when the doctor will be there. She responds that she's on her way. Within a couple of minutes the doctor comes in and introduces himself and the two nursing students he has following him that day. Claire joins us as introductions are wrapping up.

We do the breath in and breath out and he listens intently when he's in my chest area. He pulls up the X-rays and MRI scan. He walks us through what we need to do and lays out two different options. The first option is not as invasive and is essentially him sticking a needle through my chest and digging around for tissue. With the size of the mass he feels like they can get enough tissue to come up with a conclusive diagnosis but can't say for certain.

That could possibly be done tomorrow and we would have results within a day or so. The second he refers to as a Right Chamberlin and would require a little more. That's where they put you to sleep, bring in a surgeon, and go digging. They will definitely get what they need to make a diagnosis with that procedure but it would be Friday at the earliest.

After some discussion we opt for the first choice. Hopefully they will get what they need and within a couple of days we'll know exactly what we are dealing with. The unknown can be a very scary place to be and it was nice in an odd way to be able to think within a day or two we could rule out all the things that it is not and begin to focus on what it is.

I distinctly remember the two young nursing students standing in the corner. A small examining room made for two or three but holding all five of us. They were fully aware of the situation. While the doctor had decades of experience that allowed him to approach this discussion through analysis and physiology, they did not. The looks on their faces reflected their attempt—but inability—to mask their emotions as our story unfolded.

Everything was put in motion and scheduled before we left the office. Tomorrow, Wednesday, we would have the biopsy. That night and the next morning I went through the pre-op instructions that would become second nature to me. Before all this cancer nonsense it would seem like a lot to ask: No food or drink after midnight, up at 5:00 A.M., arrive at such and such time for check in, etc. How quickly it became the norm.

I did as instructed and arrived early at the hospital the next morning. I was prepped and could feel the coolness of the table on my back as I got postioned for what came next. The doctor came in and walked me through the procedure. I had some morphine a bit earlier but he explained they would also give me several shots to apply a local anesthetic to my chest area to numb it up. He said that may be a little uncomfortable. The nurse would be sitting on a stool just behind my head. Some-one from the lab would be in the room to take the samples and do a preliminary analysis to hopefully tell if they get what they need. He will go in with a needle and get a sample and hand it over to the lab person. "We probably need to do that about four times. And I need you to lay as still as you can. Any questions? Ok, here we go."

He rattled off some medical jargon to the nurse as I pre-pared for the uncomfortable shots in my chest and four deep dives. Here come the shots. Ooh, uncomfortable indeed. There are certain areas in the body that needles just shouldn't go. Your chest is one of them. As uncomfortable as it was, at least I had an idea of what to expect and that helped. We waited a couple of minutes to let the area react.

And then here comes the deep dive. The doctor hover-

-ing right over my face. In my personal space that I would learn to surrender to the medical field. Looking at that area on my chest as if double checking the winning numbers on a lottery ticket. He then holds up the needle to get it in position and I get my first glimpse at what we're dealing with.

Holy crap! This isn't going to be good. He begins to insert what is not so much a needle but a dipstick into my chest. After the initial pain of the needle he would feed it in deeper and hit nerves that have never, and should never, be stirred. Out it comes and he hands that dipstick over to the lab tech. Wow! Did that ever hurt!

I breathe, say a prayer, and scramble to my happy place. Any happy place. Any place besides right here, right now. In again. Inches from my face. I see the dipstick go in and scrape, scrape, scrape. This odd crunching sound coming from inside of me that I can feel in my teeth. Oh my goodness are you kidding me?! The drugs didn't seem to dull an ounce of it. Again. Third time. In, scrape, and out. Each part with its own unique painful sensation.

Hovering for the fourth and, thank you Lord, the final time. In, scrape, out. Wow! Breathe. Out it comes and thank God we are done. Just like on Dad's wipe board back in Ann Arbor. Checked them off. A temporary discomfort. Done. Thank you Jesus.

As I'm recovering I hear, "Hmm, yeah. ok," just off to the side of me.

And back he comes. Number five. Inches from my face again. Dipstick fed in again. Oh dear Lord! Scrape, scrape, scrape. Go to the happy place to hide. Out it comes. My body feeling hot and sweaty and the pain building. We're past my preparation point and I'm doing everything I can to keep my body still as I was instructed. My back obediently pressed against the cold table but my feet involuntarily flail around like popcorn as the needle goes in, scrapes around, and comes out.

He rolls over to the lab tech and I ask God to please get me out of here.

And he's back. He leans in for number six. I start to feel clammy and know I'm in trouble. Five was not in the plan and six is too much. It goes in. Feet flailing. Back cemented to the table.Stars erupting in my vision with my eyes shut to try to block the visual stimuli of watching. I hear alarms beeping behind me and a soft but professional female voice of the nurse at my head: "Mr. Klein? Mr. Klein are you ok?" She says something that I don't understand but recognize as a dose of something.

"Come on Dan, stay with us."

She begins to read off stats to the doctor as I succumb to the pain. The room goes dark.

Thank God when I come to I am out of that room and Claire is with me in post-op.

We found out the results the next day, Thursday. A 24 hour period in which hours and minutes painfully ticked by while waiting for results. Could it just be a noncancerous tumor? Was it indeed lymphoma or some other kind of cancer? I went to work that day. Just waiting for the phone to ring. That's a tough day to make it through. The call finally came in. The results of the biopsy were inconclusive. Damn.

The biopsy and all the pain and discomfort were for nothing. What a punch in the stomach. Through all the medical procedures and treatments and needles and you name it with cancer this first foray was by far the most physical discomfort of the entire process. I was just swallowing all of that information when, to pile on as cancer so readily does, I was told another biopsy was scheduled for the next morning. I hung up the phone and cried.

I learned two valuable lessons from that first biopsy. Lessons that would play a significant role in both enduring the grueling fight through chemotherapy and life after cancer.

First: Manage Expectations. I would never underestimate the physical side again. I would not be caught unprepared. I would absolutely not put myself in that position. I would mentally prepare for the worst case scenarios being the norm. Never again would my expectations for the extent of the physical discomfort and pain be outdone by the actual experience. Whatever complications that could arise I just expected to arise. Whatever could go wrong would go horribly wrong. Just plan on it. If by some miracle things don't go completely off the tracks than I'll take the upside surprise.

Second: The mind can exercise control over the body. The fifth and sixth trip into my chest were no different than the first four. They all hurt like hell. So why were the last two so traumatic that my body hit the off button and just shut down? If the mind could alter the body's physical state on the downside, actually influence the physiology of the body based on what it is processing, it stands to reason it can do the same on the upside.

Chapter 6:
Foundations of Faith & Family

People have said to me, both before and after cancer, that I have remarkable faith. But I can't say faith has always been easy for me. I'm not sure if faith is really easy for anyone. After all, when you stop and think about what you are really believing it is beyond rational and any level of human logic. But faith has been easier for me than for Claire and I think that has a lot to do with our experience growing up.

We were both raised Catholic. We both came from loving and caring families. While our foundation of family was very similar, we had two very different experiences in the foundation of our faith. Claire grew up in a small town in Kentucky where being Catholic certainly puts you in the minority. While she experienced faith at home, attended mass on a regular basis, and experienced the sacraments, the opportunities to engage in her faith were far fewer than mine.

Growing up in Grand Rapids, there were literally dozens of Catholic grade schools and multiple Catholic high schools. We attended St. Stephen from K-8 and went on to Catholic Central High School. After high school, Mary and I continued our Catholic education at Saint Louis University and Caroline to Notre Dame. Our faith and education went hand in hand. Be it home or at school we were always surrounded by our faith.

Mom and Dad lived out our faith both inside and, more importantly, outside the physical walls of St. Stephen. They were always involved in something. They were lecterns or Eu---

charistic ministers. They joined bible studies and prayer groups among many other ministries. After mass, they were always visiting with someone or discussing whatever project, ministry, or initiative they were involved in as we would wait impatiently and continue to ask "Can we go now?" To this day, Dad pushing 80 and Mom five years behind, at an age when many people require care from others, they still volunteer and spend the night at a homeless shelter offering whatever practical, social, and spiritual support they can.

They were as active in the school of St. Stephen as they were in the church. Dad coached basketball teams and served on the board. Mom served as a volunteer librarian and filled countless other roles—from being room Mom to helping with field trips. I have a niece and nephew who attend St. Stephen now and Mom continues her role in the library for them just as she did for us. The only difference is now she does so in the library that has been dedicated in my parent's honor and bears their names.

Growing up, missing mass on Sunday was out of the question, even on vacation. In a world before internet and iPhone apps Mom always, much to our chagrin, found a Catholic church for us to attend. Although, one time I remember it was in doubt. We were in northern Michigan skiing and got snowed in on a Sunday morning. It actually looked like we would skip mass and sleep in and find out what people who don't go to church do on Sunday mornings! But Mom, the Pope of the North as Dad calls her, would not be denied. She found mass on a new technology called cable television. That morning, snowed in, the seven of us sat in the living room for an hour going through the normal gestures of mass watching it on TV.

We always prayed before dinner. That's not so unusual. But, looking back, I appreciate the manner in which that nightly ritual unfolded. Mom—who we joke that from any picture taken from the '70s, was always in her ankle length cotton night gown because with five kids in six years she never had a chance to change during the day—would be busy preparing dinner. We all had either our before or after dinner chores. After we completed our specific chore—making salads, getting drinks, setting the table—we waited for Mom to come to the table. Nobody sat down before her. A sign of respect. We would stand behind our chairs and wait. She would finally sit down in that stained nightgown. A testament to her constant dedication to what she will tell you is her finest achievement in life—her five children—and the rest of us would follow suit.

Dad would start the blessing of the food and then we would go around the table and everyone would offer something up in prayer. Often we got away with offering a "special intention" when we couldn't or didn't want to say something specific. After dinner, Dad would get the bible and one of us would read. There would be a discussion about the passage and the meaning and lessons it provided. Through elementary school, high school, college, and beyond that was our dinner. Long after the homemade placemats and Mom's stained nightgown were gone, the ritual continued. I recognize now that our ice cream and devotion tradition is an offshoot of that dinner table experience. A valuable tradition adjusted to fit our time and our family

Claire tells the story of the first time she came to Michigan to meet my family and her first experience with the Klein family dinner tradition. As the normal dinner blessing began, she suddenly realized she had to actually participate. Not what she was expecting during her first visit to her boyfriend's family. I didn't think a thing about it and didn't think to give her a warning. It's just the way we always began dinner. Be it as a five-year-old with my "Danny" placemat or a 20-year-old bringing home this really cute girl form Kentucky. After dinner out came the bible and Claire, again not spared, made it through with flying colors as she always does with everything.

I think Claire's experience growing up was similar to a lot of people. Gail and George provided a very loving and wonderful home where she learned values and a moral code consistent with the teachings of Jesus Christ. But from a religious perspective, it may have been a bit more mechanical than spiritual or even obligatory. But while my faith foundation may have been deeper and more developed, the underpinning of the love that she experienced was second to none.

I remember the first time I visited her family. An unannounced visit at that. It was the summer between my sophomore and junior year. We had been dating for a little more than a year and I stayed in St. Louis that summer primarily to be closer to her. After not seeing her for way too long—a few weeks—I made the impromptu decision to go see her on a surprise visit. I bought a map from the Shell gas station near campus, filled up the car, and headed east across the bridge over the Mississippi River, heading to some map dot in Kentucky called Glasgow.

It was one of those things that you're all excited about but then in the middle of it you start having second thoughts. Map laid out in the passenger seat, driving through the beautiful gently rolling hills of Kentucky, I started to wonder if this was really a good idea. "This is crazy. What in the heck am I thinking? I'm just going to show up at her house? I don't even know these people. These people don't even know me. I can still turn around and be back in St. Louis in a few hours."

In the end, on that day and as it still is today, there is nothing in this world that would make me turn around from being with Claire. Excited and more than a little nervous, I rang the front doorbell. Many years from now, if some twenty-year-old boy that I barely know shows up with his bags in hand at my front door to visit Natalie I'm not exactly sure how I will respond. But I will remember—try to remember—the way I was so graciously received into their family.

I know now that Gail and George are not front door nor doorbell type of people. They are back door, knock if you want, but come on in and come as you are type of people. They are incredible people and I fell in love with their family almost as much as I fell in love with Claire. On my unannounced visit to her home, I began to connect the dots on why Claire is such an incredible person.

I was immediately welcomed into the family not because of who I am. But because of who they are. And because I was loved by their daughter. What a great lesson and a tribute to the type of people they are. While Claire may not have had the same foundation of faith that I had, she knew love. And as the reading from our wedding so accurately captures: "So faith, hope, love remain, these three. But the greatest of these is love."

Chapter 7: Second Biopsy

At the same time we are scheduling that second biopsy for Friday, Claire scheduled an appointment at Vanderbilt the following week to get a second opinion. I was relieved to find out that for Friday's biopsy they put me to sleep. After another difficult day of going about your life as if nothing is amuck and trying, mostly unsuccessfully, to sleep at night, Friday morning rolled around. I got to the hospital early on an empty stomach as I was supposed to. Claire stayed home to get the kids up and delivered to school.

By this time we had told Claire's parents what we knew. When you need to get four young children up and ready and delivered for the day it's a busy time. But more than the logistical support carrying around that type of burden and keeping it from those closest to you—for all the right reasons—is difficult. Difficult emotionally and also just practically speaking it's difficult to pull off.

Claire and her Mom speak pretty much every day. Gail has always spent at least one day a week watching one of our kids. Those who know you best know when something isn't right. Of course we didn't want to raise any false alarms in the event it wasn't cancer and even if it was, we wanted to make sure we had accurate information. But Claire and Gail are very close and we just needed her.

Claire had just joined me after dropping the kids off. It was around 8:15 on Friday morning and we're back in pre-op waiting. Last Friday at this time I was heading to church to volunteer as I do most every other Friday mornings. About a year earlier, in response to a sermon our priest gave about service and serving others, I looked for some way I could help. He suggested and challenged us to find one hour a week to volunteer for something. Just one hour.

My work schedule is pretty flexible and it worked better for me to do two hours every other week. I considered the various ministries offered through our church and opted for the Ministry of Care. This is a small group of people who make weekly visits to those who can't make it to mass for whatever reason. We go to the local nursing homes, assisted living facilities, hospitals—including the one I find myself in—as well as those who are homebound. We pray with them and, for those who can receive, bring them communion.

I chose this ministry partially because it is outside of my comfort zone. Way outside. I joke that I eased into ministry work by joining the men's softball team more than a decade earlier. As time went by Claire and I joined the baptism team followed by the couples' bible study. Then we began teaching children's liturgy during mass and later, one of our most rewarding ministries, mentoring engaged couples preparing for the sacrament of marriage.

About a year before my diagnosis, a group of guys from church who we came to know through these various activities informally starting meeting for breakfast. We just felt a need, more of a calling, to move our faith journey forward. We started meeting for breakfast every other week, working deliberately on how we are called to be better husbands, fathers and businessmen who follow the teachings of Jesus Christ.

There was a recognition in our group that there were some things going on in the world that weren't aligned with our values or faith. It was frustrating that the problems seemed so enormous there was little we could do. But we also recognized that we did have influence over some things.

There were things within our control. We had enormous influence over our families and, albeit to a much lesser extent, our professional and personal circle. And while we may never put a dent in the issues of the world individually, there was no doubt collectively we could have some impact at least in our community. A community our children would someday inherit.

I've always been blessed to be surrounded by good friends from the different stages of my life. I still keep in touch with a few of my old grade school buddies from Michigan. Every few years we seem to find a way to get together. I have eight buddies from college spread out around the Midwest and we make a point to hold our annual revival where we all come together every year with smaller gatherings sprinkled in as the opportunities arise.

Bowling Green has been no different. Friends who we vacation with or get together to go to sporting events or friends who for more than the last decade we've gotten together with to watch "Survivor." Sometimes people just get placed in your path for a reason.

I've heard it say that we are the average of the 5 people we spend the most time with. If there's any merit in that, and I don't doubt there is, we're very fortunate to surround ourselves with a lot of really good people.

One morning, at breakfast, one of the guys pointed out how involved everyone at the table was in our families, church, and communities. He started rattling off the different ministries and community involvements and it was an impressive list.

When you surround yourself with people like that I think it makes you want to do more. You support each other or, as we like to say, you lock shields together. It makes each of the parts as well as the total sum stronger. Sometimes, someone needs to lean on your for strength and support. Sometimes, you need them.

I don't suppose many people enjoy visiting nursing homes or hospitals. I certainly don't. It's uncomfortable for me to walk into a nursing home room or to ring the doorbell of an unfamiliar house in an unfamiliar neighborhood. To pray, read the gospel, and delivering communion to someone I've never met. I can now look back and see God's hand guiding me to that particular ministry to help prepare me for my own journey.

A funny thing happened the prior week after I finished my visits and made my 35 minute drive to work. There is a particular spot where every morning I turn everything off and spend about ten to fifteen minutes in prayer and silence. I thank God for the beautiful day regardless of what kind of day it is. I say prayers of gratitude for our many blessings and hand over to God things that am I struggling with and things I have no control over. I spend some time in what I have come to call the classroom of silence. And I always end the same way:

"Lord help me become the man I am called to be. Jesus, I turn my day over to you."

For some reason, I don't know why, on that day I added an extra line to my prayer after I committed that day to Jesus:

"Jesus, I turn my life over to you."

Three days after I made that offering cancer came calling. Seven days after I made that commitment I'm lying in a hospital bed waiting for biopsy #2. I'm wounded and hurt. So on this Friday morning instead of finding my way to church to get my assignments of where to visit I find myself laying in a bed at the hospital.

How quickly life can turn. How quickly you can go from being the care giver to the one in need of care. How quickly you can go from being the one standing on the side of the hospital bed offering to the one laying in the hospital bed needing. How quickly you can go from being perfectly able to stand and pray and visit and empathize and then turn right around and walk right out the door and on with your life.

Walking out the door is not an option on this day. As I'm lying there waiting for the biopsy I decide to text my friend Leslie who also delivers communion through that ministry.

Me: You doing MOC today??

Leslie:Yes, running late but on my way.

I pause not sure if I really want to—or am ready to— open the door to the outside world. But if anyone would understand it's Leslie. She went through cancer a couple of years before. Her kids are similar in age to ours. I know Leslie enough to say hello to her when I see her but I don't know her really that well. During Leslie's battle with cancer Claire sent her cards and during her treatment when they moved their family to Houston, TX for a couple of months Claire sent her zoo passes and some other thoughtful things for the kids. That's just Claire.

Me: Can you request the MedCenter?

Leslie: Sure, anyone there in particular you want me to see?

I pause again. Claire and I are pretty private people I like to think. In this day and age of posting your dinner plate and your daily activities on Facebook we just do our thing. We don't really worry about what other people think. We just focus on our family. I know Leslie will understand and will keep it confidential.

Me: Actually, me. Had something show up on an Xray and having a biopsy. Getting ready to go in. Claire will be in the waiting room.

Leslie: I'm on my way!! I'll be there as soon as I can. I'll be praying.

At that point a nurse came in to check my vitals. She walked in and from her body language I could tell she was towards the end of her long night shift. She begins to rattle of the usual questions "Name?" I respond. "Date of birth?" I pause just a moment and swallow hard.

This process, giving my name and date of birth, became an emotional trigger point for me through the first several weeks. Every time you check in for a procedure or go into a different doctor's office or waiting room they ask you your name. Every time a new nurse or doctor comes in they identify you by asking you "date of birth." Then they either put on or check your wrist bracelet.

Saying my name and date of birth and sticking my wrist out to get that band on or checked made it all very real. It wasn't just in my head and it wasn't just a really bad dream. I could not just turn and walk right out the door back to my life.

I would give or confirm my name and date of birth and try to maintain my composure as best I could as that trigger fired. Then as they had done umpteen times that shift they would look at the patient's chart and see what they are dealing with. This particular nurse stood at the bottom of my bed and as she read through my chart her body language changed. Her shoulders and face dropped just enough to be noticeable.

"You're here for a biopsy?"

I just nod because I'm still recovering from the name and date of birth reaction. She looks back at the chart. "You had another biopsy as well on Wednesday?" I tell her it didn't work. "How long have you been dealing with this?" "Monday." Her shoulders and face drop and her tone changes. She understands what is going on.

She closes the chart.

"Ok honey, here's what we're going to do" as she pulls a stool up next to my bed. Even though she's been on her feet for twelv hours and is probably anxious to get out the door, she recognizes I'm scared and hurt. She puts her hand on my arm and in a tone more suited to a mother than a nurse walks me through the procedure. She stays with me the next fifteen minutes as I get prepped.

The anesthesiologist comes in.

"Name and date of birth?" Trigger. She begins to question him more for my sake because she, of course, already knows the answers.

"Now, when you give him the good stuff it will be lights out right?"

"That's right. You'll remember being rolled down the hall and the next thing you'll know you'll be waking up in recovery. All finished."

In comes the surgeon and introduces himself.

"Mr. Klein, I'm Dr. Moore. Name and date of birth please?"

He checks my wrist band and asks me what we're doing today.

"A Right Chamberlin," I say.

"And why are we doing that?" He asks.

"For a biopsy."

She asks him, "and you guys are sure you'll get what you need on this one?"

"Yup, we'll know what we're dealing with."

She looks at me with a smile and a gesture to make sure I understand.

"Ok, Mr. Klein, do you have any questions?"

Boy do I ever have questions. Just none that he can answer.

"No sir. I'm ready."

With that the anesthesiologist plugs the good stuff into my IV and they begin to roll me out of the room. We begin that short and awkward exposed commute of laying in a hospital bed as you get wheeled down the halls and around corners. The nurse is walking next to me as we turn into the operating room. We enter a small room with very bright lights and several people in gowns and masks waiting.

I begin to feel very cozy.

In the last four days I haven't had much sleep and my body is running on fumes. It feels good to know sleep is on the way and that when I wake up this whole biopsy mess is behind me. I look around the room and begin to slowly blink as the anesthesia circulates through my body. The nurse is still next to me. Her hand on my arm. "You're going to be ok" is the last thing I remember her saying.

Chapter 8: Coming Out of the Closet

For me, I can sum up biopsies by just saying you don't ever want one. You get a piece of you carved out to be analyzed. That's the physical part and that's no fun. Then you add the emotional and psychological stress. And the accompanying cruel waiting period. A few days where you stand idly by and attempt to go through the motions of your life. Your mind puts you through a period of torment as it wanders through the worst possible scenarios. In an odd way this window of torment can be worse than cancer itself. At least when you have your diagnosis you can eliminate a lot of scary scenarios and only deal with one.

The initial results from my second biopsy confirmed it was Hodgkin's lymphoma. That's what we thought it was and what we were hoping for. There's some more sub classifications that need to be done but we are narrowing the range of possibilities. Hodgkin's lymphoma has the best survival odds out of the other potential cancers we were looking at, around a 90% survival rate. We're fortunate to have something we can deal with.

Claire is busy arranging a second opinion at Vanderbilt. We are doing our best to go about our work and home life and trying to sort out the logistics as we go. When we were first making the arrangements at Vandy they wanted all the records we had to this point so they could review and analyze. I was especially hoping the information from the first two biopsies would suffice for their diagnosis. But they wanted to do their own biopsy. Not just any biopsy. A bone marrow biopsy. I'm talking with Sean two days before we go to Vandy and mention to him about having the bone marrow biopsy.

"Ooh." He says.

"What?" I ask.

No response.

"What??" I repeat.

"Dan, that's the mother of all biopsies."

Not what I wanted to hear. I begin to put into practice my early lessons about managing expectations. This is going to hurt. This is going to be really bad. And I have two days to think about this. That's not good.

We also need to notify our family and our friends. It's a tough conversation and one you don't want to have. I ask Claire if it's something we can just deal with and not tell anyone until it all blows over. Not out of embarrassment or shame. That's not it. More out of the stigma of cancer and to defer the sheer ultimate logistics that come with telling others about it. And maybe to stay in any part of denial we have left.

Claire's too smart for that. "That's not how cancer works. Eventually people will know and we're going to need help. And people are going to want to help us. We would want to help someone else." She was so right. She always is.

My parents happen to be coming through town, on their way to Florida from Michigan for the winter. After church on Sunday the kids went to their classes and we pulled Mom and Dad into a side room. I know as a parent there is no pain like the pain of seeing your child hurt. Regardless of your age, it's tough to tell your Mom & Dad that their child has cancer.

Later that afternoon while Natalie napped—she was only four and thankfully could be spared this conversation— we sat the boys down on the couch in the playroom and had the difficult discussion.

When I see someone smoking or chewing tobacco I immediate remember that scene and the emotion and think "Buddy, if you only knew what I knew you'd quit right now." Regardless of the torment cancer can put you through, why on earth would you do anything that would increase the chance of putting yourself in that position to hurt the people you love.

Next is our siblings and then our friends. It's a long and emotionally, psychologically, and physically exhausting process. And nobody knows what to say. Of course they don't. I never did either. For you it's the 10th or 15th or 20th call you've made and you're tired, but you also respect that the person you are calling is hearing it for the first time.

Every conversation is a little different but everyone is the same. "I am so sorry. If there's anything, anything you need call me. Night or day. You know my cousin had cancer . . ."

And here comes the cancer story. The dreaded cancer story. A human phenomena known to those in the cancer club. I've heard everyone's cancer story. Their cousin, their grandmother, their brother. It's an understood nuisance among the membership and our conversation goes like this: "When you told people about your diagnosis did you hear their cancer stories?" "Oh that's the worst! Hearing everyone's cancer story! "

The only ones you typically don't hear the stories from are those who have had cancer. They understand. They know you are just trying to deal with one cancer story. Your cancer story. Piling others on top despite the good intentions is extra weight at a time when there is no more weight to bear.

I also didn't appreciate the whole "You'll beat this thing" and "You're going to be just fine" commentary. My external response was a head nod and a quiet thank you. My internal response was how the heck do you know? Who told you? Because I don't know that. Maybe for some people that positive encouragement is appreciated, it makes sense, but for whatever reason to me it was just so frustrating. They could say the words so easily and without cost or risk but the path was so uncertain and daunting.

The bottom line is people don't know what to say or what to do. I did the same thing. You want to say something to make them feel better. But what do you say to someone who tells you they just found out they have cancer?

Here's what you say: I am so sorry that you have to deal with this. Please know you and your family will be in my prayers. Is there someone I can get in touch with about doing something that will help you?

Here's what you do: Contact that point person if such a person exist. If not, offer to be that person to arrange and coordinate things that they need. Send them cards, notes, or even a gift card for a meal. Do it frequently. Mark your calendar and know their schedule. Know when they are going for treatment. Know when the scan is. Every few weeks take 5 minutes for them. You don't have to write something profound. Just let them know you are thinking and praying for them.

And do pray. It's part of the mystery of this life. For me it's my faith in our heavenly Father. Others may refer to it as karma or positive energy or just good vibes. Regardless, in the quiet of your heart raise them up often. Set aside a portion of your day, even just half an hour while you work or you're with your family, and dedicate it to them and pour yourself into it for their struggle. Consciously take advantage of every second of that time and live it for them knowing they don't have that luxury. Begin or add to a positive habit like exercising or going to mass during the week. Or stop a negative habit. And let them know about it. It's one of those spiritual things that I can't explain. It's why we call it faith and not fact. That positive energy transfer I would get from that text from a friend telling me the next hour they were working for me. Or they ran an extra mile that day just for me. Or the card thanking me for inspiring them to get off the couch, sign up, train, and complete a triathlon because they knew their old friend was struggling to just get out of bed. Or that after years of trying they finally quit chewing tobacco. You can't measure the impact of those things.

Everyone handles cancer differently. Some people are more private than others. Some people don't want to or know how to ask or even how to accept help. For us we knew we had to accept help. What we told our close friends was that we needed them. Now more than ever. We know you don't know what to say or do and that's ok because neither do we. But we know we need you. We need your love and support. And it would be better for you to push in too much than to pull back. If you're pushing in too much we will tell you. Please don't be offended and we won't either. But we can't have you moving away. Not now. We need you.

So with our family and friends locked in and their support both locally and long distance our support system began to take form. We didn't know what lay ahead of us but knew who stood with us. That part we could control. We made darn sure we had the right people in the right seats on that bus.

The Bridge

NOTE TO READER*

I've said it before, but I think it's important to repeat: I'm not much of a social media user. I suppose I'd rather be putting my energy and time into living my life rather than posting a version of my life online that I think I want you to see. Claire has a Facebook page but never made a single post about our life with cancer. It honestly just didn't seem like the right format for us.

But then CaringBridge happened to us, and I slowly realized the power of an online community. CaringBridge is a website that was designed specifically for people going through health issues. Claire had followed our friend Leslie's ordeal with cancer via CaringBridge and then my Dad used a similar site with his cancer fight. It's an easy and efficient communication tool.

What follows are posts written as we travelled on our journey—with a few off ramps, as I reflect on those posts. Here and there, I've edited for clarity, but for the most part the words you'll read in "The Bridge" are how they were posted. At times, Claire steps in—as she did on CaringBridge—when words were too much for me, or my partner needed to carry me and the message for a little bit, but throughout, you'll get a glimpse of our journey as it happened, as I struggled to make sense of it all, and struggled to reach my own 3:59.

*For a look at the complete CaringBridge account visit CaringBridge.org and search "Dan Klein."

Welcome to CaringBridge:
Our Story By Dan Klein, Jan 23, 2014

After 5-6 weeks of what started as a very mild cough that kept hanging around and getting a bit worse, I dropped the kids off at school and called my doctor one Monday morning. That was January 13th. I got into the doctors' office and did the usual. Thankfully, Paul's training and instincts led him to have a breathing test performed in the office and had me go get a chest X-ray. About an hour later, I was back in his office looking at the X-rays, as he informed me of a mass in my chest area that was cancer.

Thank you again, Paul, for your masterful blend of friend and physician in delivering that news. The next time I have to wait in a doctor's office for some routine trip, I will just thank God that I'm not the one the doctor is having to spend extra time talking with and coordinating CT scans and blood work and who knows what else.

There's a lot that has happened since that day. Suffice to say it has been a difficult time.

The bad news is I have cancer but—other than that—everything has been positive. If you're going to get dealt the cancer card this one is high on the list. What I have is Hodgkin's lymphoma. It takes the form of a mass about the size of a grapefruit and is between my chest and my lungs. Survival rate is very high. I'm young, in good health otherwise, active, and don't smoke, so all of those help.

Treatment will consist of chemo and possibly radiation. I've been told 4-6 months of treatment. My chemo port will be implanted in my chest this Friday. I will say, I'm growing tired of getting sharp instruments poked through my chest.

As a Christian, I can find peace with this however this ends. I'm very thankful for my Catholic faith and the wonderful faith community at Holy Spirit. But as a husband and father, a son and brother, and friend it's more complicated.

God has blessed us in so many ways through the life we have. After two weeks of dealing with this, I came to realize this morning during my morning prayer time that my prayer life really hasn't changed since the diagnosis. I'm certainly praying more frequently throughout the day and for the specifics of the situation and for others in this situation with my new perspective. But I take it as a positive that my conversations with God really haven't changed.

The biggest blessing in our life is our four kids. I learned that first afternoon after finding out I have cancer, your children still need homework reviewed, need to eat, be cleaned, disputes resolved, put to bed, etc. I also learned the mail keeps coming and the plumbing can go bad.

Life around you stays in motion despite you standing still. So, you take a step and off you go. It takes a lot to run a house with 4 active kids even with 2 engaged, willing, and loving adults who can focus primarily on them. But when you dump the stress of cancer invading your home and one parent going through chemo there is a lot of slack that needs to be picked up.

We know without asking you, our family and friends, will circle the wagons and pick up that slack without hesitating. Thank you in advance. Old and new friends. And friends we will come to know and know better through this ordeal. We know we will have a lot of needs. We just dont know exactly what those are right now. So if you are willing to assist in this battle on whatever scale we will accept your help. We hope to have some system in place to facilitate that, so Claire and I can focus on the kids and getting better.

There are two things that we would ask of you to do right now and that we ask if you start you don't stop until the word "Cured" is plastered all over this sight. That may be six months or longer so give this some thought before you start.

1.) I start every morning by reading a chapter of Proverbs and then sitting quietly for about five minutes or so and listening for any thoughts God may want to put in my head. Proverbs is basically a blue print for how you should live your life. There are 31 chapters in Proverbs so if you read one each day for most months you will read just one a day. Other months you pick up an extra here or there. On the first of the next month you just start over again and you go back to chapter one. It takes about 3-4 minutes at most. So tomorrow is the 26th and I will start my morning routine by lighting my candle, putting on the coffee, and reading Proverbs 26. I then will spend about five minutes in what I have come to know as "the classroom of silence".

If you are up for giving me 5-10 minutes of your morning for the next 6 months or so that's what you can do for me. If you find a line or a thought that stands out or speaks to you please share with me.

2.) As some of you may be aware the Kleins are known for their love of ice cream. Every night we have our ice cream as sure as the sun rises and sets. On the suggestion of some friends we bought the book *Jesus Calling 365 Devotions for Kids*. We all sit down at the kitchen table with our ice cream, light the candle, and take turns reading that day's devotion. We then each take turns discussing what we thought about that devotion or a phrase or word that spoke to us. It has been amazing since the diagnosis how the devotions have spoken directly to exactly what we were dealing with that day. Finally, we each go around and say something, big or small, that we are thankful for that day.

If you want to do something for me, go buy that book and sit down with your family or sit down with just God and read the daily devotion and reflect on what it means to you. For those of you without kids there's a *Jesus Calling for Adults* but we love the kids one so much we just stick with that.

My faith is very important to me but I tend to keep it more private than public. Rather than have a bumper sticker or a billboard praising God I choose to adopt the style often credited to St. Francis of Assisi: Preach the gospel. Use words when necessary.

Trip to Vandy

By Dan Klein — Jan 28, 2014 6:17am

This morning we head to Nashville to see David Morgan who is a specialist in leukemia & lymphoma for a seconnd opinion. Our hope is the diagnosis is the same. That would confirm what we are dealing with is manageable and may lead us to stay in Bowling Green for treatment.

They have all the different test that we've done but want to do a bone marrow biopsy as well. We're scheduled for some blood work at 8:40 and then to see the doc at 9:30 and then the biopsy is scheduled for 12:00. I have a new found respect for people who go through biopsies.

Treatment consist of chemo and possibly radiation—but it may just be chemo. If we need to do both then we'll do both. I am scheduled Friday morning to have my chemo port put in my chest. And then we are probably looking at the week of Feb. 3rd or Feb. 10th to get this show on the road. I am ready. We'll just have to see how my body reacts. Hopefully it is mild but regardless it's the path to being cured and it needs to be done.

So say a pray for me while you are eating your lunch for the biopsy and say a pray of thanksgiving this evening with your dinner that this part is behind us and ask for good results.

I borrowed a quote from yesterday's Proverbs 27:17

Iron sharpens iron, and one man sharpens another.

My Baby Face
By Dan Klein — Jan 28, 2014 8:53am

The day started out well here at Vandy. We went to register and I gave the lady, Miss Fannie, our last name. She looked a bit at her screen and said "Hmm, I see a Daniel but that can't be you. You're much too young for that date of birth." I thanked her and said "That's me." and she said, "You sure don't look 40! More like 20!"

Off to a good start.

Done and Heading Home
By Dan Klein — Jan 28, 2014 2:16 pm

We really liked the doctor. We sat with him and his side-kick for about 45 minutes. Answered a lot of questions and laid out what we can expect. Waiting on some final path work and the biopsy reports from today to finalize diagnosis.

Due to the size of the mass he categorized it as stage two. Not great news, but we can deal with it. We really need the bone marrow biopsy to come back showing nothing in the bones. But if it does, we'll need to back up a step and regroup. We really didn't go into that in depth because his guess was it would come back clean.

January 29th
By Dan Klein — Jan 29, 2014

We greatly appreciate the posts and emails/cards/texts. I cannot express enough our appreciation.

We were back to Graves Gilbert today for a second visit with Dr. Smith, who is the oncologist here in BG. He has been fantastic as have the people in his office. They have bent over backwards to get us taken care of and we greatly appreciate that. With that being said, we have made the decision to be treated by Dr. David Morgan, at Vanderbilt, who is a specialist in Hodgkin's lymphoma and will begin chemo next Wednesday.

Chemo will be every two weeks for six months. After two months, another PET scan will be done, and we'll get our first look to see if the chemo is doing the trick.

If it's working and the cancer is going away, the outlook is very positive. If not, that's not a real good sign and the chemo would be adjusted. After chemo, we'll do a month of radiation—five days a week for four weeks. That puts us through August, believe it or not. I'm thinking some major Labor Day party is in order, so mark your calendars!

The bone marrow biopsy was better than I expected. Thank you to Leslie who did the biopsy and did an outstanding job. I'd like to say I hardly knew she was digging bone out. She's good. But not that good. But it was much better than I mentally planned for.

And I appreciate her letting me in on the secret "RBR Positive" code. As I was lying on the very short table waiting —I think the same person designed airplane seats and hotel showers—Dr. Morgan poked his head in and asked about RBR Positive?? They did a little exchange. He nodded and closed the door.

I waited a moment trying to process what the heck they were talking about. Crap, I tested positive for some other kind of weird thing called RBR?!?

Finally I said "Ok, what the heck is RBR Positive?" Leslie smiled as she was focusing on the large needle she was tapping and said "There's a Mexican place across the street and every other Tuesday they have a red beans and rice special. So "RBR Positive??" is code for "do you want the red beans and rice special??"

Thank you, Lord, for injecting a little humor when I needed it.

So the last big hurdle of this stage of the process is waiting for the bone marrow biopsy results. We've had such good results to this point and we just need that one more test to come back showing nothing in the bones. That's a significant one.

Other than being exhausted I feel great. We have four kids so we're kind of used to being exhausted. I'd love to start working out again and as soon as my chest heals, I plan on being back at D1 with a modified regiment.

When I do the boot camp workout, I usually wear a shirt from one of our Klein family reunions. Typically, they are an awful color like pea green, so in a crowd at an amusement park or ballpark, it's easy to spot a family member.

I wear that because when I get pushed to my limit I think of my Dad, who last year was diagnosed with gum cancer that spread into his jaw bone. He had major, major surgery and has had a very tough road that makes my challenge look like a walk in the park. His faith and attitude is something that has inspired me but not surprised me. When I work out or when I'm at work, or doing something with my family and past my limit, I figure if my Dad can battle that kind of cancer, I can find something extra in me and do one more rep or push myself a little bit harder. Thanks Dad. :)

So we wait until Friday to hear results and then start adjusting to our life with chemo. Thanks for all the prayers, love, and support. We feel them. We appreciate them. We need them.

Sacrament of Annointing
By Dan Klein — Jan 30, 2014

For those who are available, we welcome you to join us at Holy Spirit Catholic Church at 6:00 on Monday, February 3rd, for the sacrament of the anointing.

We await the news from the bone marrow biopsy tomorrow but really don't expect any surprises. To be honest I haven't given it much thought the last couple of days. That would be a game changer. But both doctors, BG and Vandy, essentially said the probability is so small they don't expect anything in there. If they don't, I don't.

I feel great other than being tired. The cough that lead to the initial diagnosis is still a bit difficult to deal with at night as the mass sits on my lungs when I lay down. Sorry again, Claire, for all the coughing. Between the cough and the incisions of the different biopsies still healing it's just hard to get comfortable.

Tomorrow, hopefully, wraps up our diagnosis phase of this process and then we can begin the next phase—treatment. That's good because I've diagnosed myself with "SIF"—sharp instrument fatigue. I'm ready to get the show on the road.

The devotion we read the day I was told I had cancer, January 13th, from *Jesus Calling* was titled "Expect Surprises!" and the second paragraph reads:

"Expect surprises! When you live your life with Me, no day will ever be boring or predictable. Don't take the easiest path. Don't just get through the day. Live it! Be willing to follow Me wherever I lead. Even when My way seems scary, the safest place to be is by My side."

My response to that is, "Speak Lord your servant is listening."

Good News
By Claire Klein — Jan 31, 2014 2:06pm

Funny what good news is these days. The bone marrow biopsy was negative meaning no signs of lymphoma in the marrow. Dan can stay a stage II. If it had been positive, his HLc (Hodgkin's lymphoma) would be staged a IV.

His diagnosis is Nodular Sclerosing HL (Hodgkin's lymphoma) stage II Bulky Disease. The first time Dan has ever been called "bulky" in his life. This is the most common type (good news) and the majority of people are cured with no recurrence.

As many know, or can discover by Dan's post, he is a man of great faith. We will rely heavily on God and our family and friends during this tough time. As Dan's wife and friend, it breaks my heart for him, our family, and our friends. What you see, is what you get. I don't know a better man than Dan Klein!

We will fight this disease with a vengeance!

Thank you to everyone who has reached out to us and to those of you who have us in your prayers.

We are forever grateful,

Claire

Note from Claire: "Preserving Their Innocence"

It was a dark, dreary day and I was walking in the cold rain with the boys to my van when my cell rang. As I loaded the boys up, Paul gingerly told me, "Claire, I don't know how to tell you this, but Dan has cancer." My heart began to pound. He told me that an X-ray revealed a mass, and they were running a MRI to determine if it was in his lungs. He would call me asap with the results. Was I just told that my husband and best friend has cancer? No way could this be true! I stood in the rain and hadn't a clue what to do next. I couldn't reach Dan, and I had no one to talk to. We arrived home and I immediately called my other favorite person, my mom. When I told her, she was as shocked as I was. I told her, "I should have known that Dan Klein was too good to be true."

Dan eventually came home. He told me that we shouldn't tell anyone until we knew what we were dealing with. It was too late for that. But, of course, my mom and dad would become two of our biggest supporters.

My mom kept Natalie one day a week and had her that day at their home about 30 miles away. I drove to our meeting spot in Smith's Grove. As I left the neighborhood, Tim McGraw's "Live Like You are Dying" came on the radio. The night before, John, our oldest, had left a precious note in our room telling us what wonderful parents he had, the amazing opportunities he has had, and how much he loved us. Funny how these little things become something bigger. A reminder to us that you never know how your simple acts of kindness and love affect others. And to this day, Dan uses John's note as a bookmark in his Bible.

Mom and Natalie got in my van. We sat in stunned

silence and a few tears as Natalie jabbered on about her day. As we were sitting there, my cell rang. Paul was calling to say the good news was the mass wasn't in his lungs. I was hoping the good news was that this was a terrible mistake.

And then I felt that my life was forever changed. And in some ways it has. The next couple of weeks were a whirlwind of doctors visits and tests. Dan's unsuccessful needle biopsy, which was very uncomfortable, caused a vagal response. His heart rate and blood pressure dropped dangerously low. The results of the biopsy were inconclusive and two days later he had to be put under for a more invasive procedure. This was the hardest time of our lives. We were going through our normal paces of life with this heavy burden on our shoulders, and no one had a clue what we were going through. It makes you wonder what the person sitting next to you might have on their plate. I went to work each day with a smile on my face, crying inside.

Every night, Dan and I have always snuggled with each of our kids at bedtime. Just a few minutes and usually more. We talk to them about their day, anything else that might spring into their minds and maybe a little back scratching. We tell them how much we love them. But now, the thought that we were soon to be rocking their little worlds and telling them their dad had cancer was overwhelming. All we wanted to do was preserve their innocence. I would snuggle with the boys first, talking to keep my mind off the months—and possible years—to come. I would lie down with Natalie last. I would silently lie there in the dark crying, holding in my sobs. She loved her daddy so much. They have the sweetest relationship. Would he be here to walk her down the aisle? If he were to die, would she remember him?

The day of our first oncology appointment it snowed. Natalie got up late for preschool and to ease the transition, her sweet daddy went outside and built her a mini snowman. He brought it to her in bed on a plate. Thinking about moments like these really hurt my heart!

And then, selfishly, I would think of myself. I could manage the twins, but John really needed his daddy. He was eleven and wise beyond his years. Natalie being the emotional female in the family needed a strong male presence.

At night, Dan and I would cling to each other and watch the time go by unable to sleep.

We finally decided to tell the boys. Natalie was too young to include in the conversation. We had been planning our summer trip out west for about two to three months. We were watching movies and had laminated a map and were marking our way. After we told them, John being older and wiser, cut right to the chase and asked if Dan was going to die. It seemed so unfair for a child to be faced with this. Matthew asked if our trip out west was canceled. John said it was ok if we didn't go out west as long as Dan was cured. There were no words to capture the emotion or raw innocence of these children.

Thank You
By Dan Klein — February 1, 2014

At some point that first week, I asked Claire if we could just not tell anybody and just deal with it ourselves. Her reply was that was not how cancer worked. We were going to need logistical help and moral support. She was right. Of course she was right.

I understand now. I can't express enough how much I appreciate and am overwhelmed by the love and support that we have received. On one hand we need it and on the other hand it seems like a lot of fuss over something that is serious but manageable. In some ways I feel like the last guy to walk onto Normandy Beach on D-Day and be comforted about how terrible the day was.

There are others who have so much more serious illnesses who receive so much less support. I'm aware of my diagnosis and prognosis and if it was something different Im not sure just how well I would be holding up.

Yesterday we officially came out of the closet with our illness and bad news travels fast. There are people who we would have preferred to let know ourselves in our own words rather than finding out through an email or from someone else. That's just the way communication works these days and that's ok. To those people: thank you for your understanding of the situation.

This weekend my plan is to convert the upstairs playroom to the man cave recovery room. I will be covering the walls with the emails and posts and cards. That's my bulletin board material. Keep it coming because to this point it's been more of a mental game and short term discomfort. Chemo has been moved to Thursday and that's when the physical battle will rage and my mental game will be tested. As the cumulative effects pile up come May and June and July I'm going to find out if I can put into practice what I preach. I'm not sure that I can.

To borrow a thread from Alanis Morissette (she's a singer Mom—call me and I'll explain): I'm strong but I'm weak. I'm confident but I'm scared. I can stand up strong but I can roll up in a ball in the corner. I've laughed and I've cried. I can lead but sometimes I need to just follow.

Nice Weekend
By Dan Klein — February 2, 2014

Proverbs 2:7-8

"He reserves his advice for the honest, a shield to those whose ways are sound; he stands guard over the paths of equity, he keeps watch over the way of those faithful to him."

How do you have a bad day when you start with that??

My takeaway from last night's *Jesus Calling* devotion was pretty straight forward. We can't focus on the mountains and peaks of our lives that are so immense. But rather we focus on the path in front of us. Just focus on today. Let me be the best I can at what I'm doing today.

I'm starting to build my iTunes playlist. My song today was Journey, "Don't Stop Believing."

I start chemo on Thursday and my plan is to try to do a couple of modified workouts this week leading up to that.

Then the game plan is to resume normal activities as I can. My cough is 90% better than it was four days ago. Keep the prayers coming.

I've always known I've been blessed with great friends at every stage of my life. Add to that a strong immediate and extended family and it's been remarkable to feel and see the support. It's just not adequate but I can't help but offer a simple and humble thank you.

Goalrilla
By Dan Klein — February 2, 2014

John's birthday is December 4th and this year we wanted to get a "Goalrilla" basketball system bought and installed. Black Friday—back in November—we went online to buy it at a sales price but the shipping was going to be as much as the discount. So Claire called the store in BG to see if 1) they would give us the same price and 2) do they have it in stock.

No problem—got it ordered and paid for installation. The manager said we should be called by the Monday after Thanksgiving to set up installation. Great. Tuesday rolled around and we hadn't heard anything. I was in the neighborhood of Dick's so I stopped by to check on it and spoke with a different manager.

No problem—we'll get that taken care of for you. That night I got an email from the company they use to do the installs and I learned that they didnt do them in KY until April because of the weather. What—April??

So I went back in the next week and was very nice and explained the situation to manager #3. He was very sorry and he would see if they could get one of the local install crews who he knew to do it and he will call me back. Ok great.

Another week goes by and I don't hear anything. So I call and talk with manager #4. Explain what's going on and he assures me he will get it taken care of and call me back within the hour with an update. Nothing.

Christmas rolls in, New Years rolls in. Cancer rolls in. So it's yesterday, February 1st—2 months+ after we bought it and almost 2 months since John's birthday. When we told our friends the Loves—Nat & Cindy—about our diagnosis and Cindy said if there's something they can do to let them know, I jokingly said do you know anyone who can install a Goalrilla basketball system. Knowing full well that Nat could because Nat can build or fix anything.

We're in the kitchen yesterday morning and Cindy calls Claire and asks if we were serious. Well, yeah but we need to see if Dick's has it. So I go to Dick's to see about the Goalrilla. Claire says if I need to play the cancer card to get this thing moving, play it.

So I walk into Dick's and I know the drill. The little girl says welcome to Dick's, I say I've been trying to get a Goalrilla system installed and have had some issues, and she calls up the manager. To this point I've been very kind and patient and don't have any plans on changing that (sugar before vinegar, right Dad?).

So after a few minutes here comes manager #5. I explain to him I ordered this on Black Friday, I have spoken with several different people about it and no one has followed up. I have a friend who has offered to install it and I'd just like to get the system and get refunded the install fee and

I'll stick it in my garage and at some point we'll install it. I give him the order number and he starts plugging it in and it's not showing up and he says it's not in the system but he can look it up by my credit card.

So, following my wife's advice, which is always a wise thing to do, I say very calmly and kindly, "Sure, but here's the thing. I found out recently I have cancer and next week I start chemotherapy. I'd like to be able to watch my boys play basketball."

Within 5 minutes they found my order and there just happens to be one in stock and they are wheeling that baby out the front door. I got a gift card and a new olympic shirt for my troubles and Nat is pulling up in his truck to load it up.

That's a pretty good story in itself, but the incredible part is that Nat and Daniel Moran spent all day on Saturday digging the hole, mixing the cement, and getting the first phase of the job done while we went to the kids sporting events and took care of other things. They wouldn't let me do a thing—probably for reasons having more to do with my lack of mechanical abilities more so than cancer.

I had pretty much forgotten about the hoop and the last thing I expected was for those guys to give me their Saturday on no notice and use their skills, expertise, and kindness to make it happen. It was both a wonderful gesture of friendship as well as an incredible lesson that we were able to share with our kids about the kindness of friends.

Thanks to the Loves and Morans. Your gesture will never be forgotten.

Man Cave Accomplished
By Dan Klein — February 2, 2014

Thanks to some of my Fratres in Christos, the man cave recovery room mission is complete. Thanks guys. Fratres in Christos is Latin for brothers in Christ. It's the name our Wednesday morning breakfast group has adopted. We gather at 6:00 am every other Wednesday at Teresa's and use a side room.

We started with the book *The Resolution of Men* and for many of us was a real game changer. It's about how God calls men to be the fathers and husbands that He wants us to be. Often in contrast to popular culture and the easy way out of our responsibilities it challenged us to be the spiritual and moral leaders of our families.

A phrase from the book that we have adopted as our mantra is "locking shields." We lock shields with each other to make us all stronger. We come together to pray, pick books to read and discuss to make us better men, discuss life and our families, laugh, and recently cry.

We've committed one Sunday a month to set aside as Family Sundays and take turns planning the day. Just a chance to bring our families together. At breakfast we talk about how there are things in the world that we don't agree with and rather than shrug it off and shake our heads about the world and our country and all the things that are out of our control we focus on what we can control.

We control ourselves and our families. We can make an impact, however small, by starting in our homes with ourselves, our spouses, and our kids. I can't change the world but I have tremendous influence on the six people in my house. That's where I start. That's where I suggest you start.

We have plenty of chairs open and we hope to fill those with other like minded people. This Wednesday at 6:00 at Teresa's. First room on your right.

I believe that this illness I have been dealt to deal with has very little to do with me and a lot to do with others.

Annointing
By Dan Klein — February 3, 2014

Thank you to all who came to the anointing this evening. On short notice to take time out of your schedules I greatly appreciate the standing room only crowd. Didn't expect that. But I'm learning not to be surprised by the kindness and support of this community.

The Rumble in the Jungle
By Dan Klein — February 5, 2014

I was asked if I could post what I said from the Sacrament of Annointing. It wasn't something I had written out beforehand but more of a framework of what I wanted to express. So this won't be exact but I'll try to capture the gist of it.

And I started the same way I will today—thank you.

Thank you for the kindness shown to my family. The love and support we have received has been difficult to take in if that makes sense.

Claire and I have had somewhat of a theological debate over the years about why certain things happen. My opinion has been that God has a plan. Her opinion has been that sometimes things just happen and God would not want a husband and father of four small children to be afflicted with cancer just to make a point.

I have some new found perspective over the last few weeks and as any wise husband would do I am going to agree with her.

I have learned some things that God is and some things that God is not.

God is not cancer. Nor is He war or famine. God is not a horrific house fire. Nor is He a car accident or any of the unthinkable acts people do to each other every day. That is physiology and genetics. That is probability and physics. That is the imperfectness of the human world we live in.

God is in each of us. He dwells in our hearts and tries to reveal himself every day in acts of love and kindness and respect. Sometimes we allow Him to manifest through us and other times we oppress Him for whatever reason.

God is a phone call from a friend who was behind you in the drop off line at school. Who called and had no idea what you were dealing with on the day after you found out you had cancer. Just to tell you how beautiful your children are and how much he enjoys seeing the love and joy of your family.

God is a nurse wheeling you back for a biopsy who sees the hurt and pain and fear in your eyes and changes her tone just a bit and pats you on the arm and tells you its going to be ok.

God is you stepping onto a bus 23 years ago at the corner of Spring and Vandeventer in St. Louis when you had no intention of stepping on that bus and tried everything you could to get out of it. Only to meet the woman who would become your wife and best friend who you know you are not worthy of her love but she loves you anyways.

I know that's God. And I know my diagnosis and prognosis. I know when I stepped into the oncologist's office for the first time and looked around the waiting room and saw the pamphlets of all the different kinds of cancers I realized immediately I was the luckiest guy in the room and there wasn't a soul in there with cancer who wouldn't trade places with me in a heartbeat.

I basically have one weapon in this battle and its resolve. I'll let the doctors take care of the medicine part, lean on family and friends for love and support, and raise the rest up to God. My job is when I get knocked down, which I surely will, I got to get back up to my feet.

That's where you come in. The cards and the post and the guestbook entries. Those are my bulletin board material. I appreciate everyone and will need them.

I know my opponent. I know what he looks like. I know what he smells like. And I know what he feels like—a warm suffocating heat. I have named and renamed my opponent a few times waiting to settle on the right name to capture him.

My first name was inappropriate. Let's just say it was a compound word and started with an "A" and ended with an "E". Being a Michigan fan I considered Buckey—but I reconsidered. I wanted something simple. Something that would stand as a symbol for who I was fighting. I then went with George for reasons listed below. But George is too much of an important name in our family to associate with anything bad.

In 1974 Muhammed Ali fought George Foreman in what Don King promoted as the "Rumble in the Jungle." After the first round Ali realized Foreman was too strong. Too big and too overpowering. Ali knew he couldnt match the power. So he switched tactics.

For rounds 2-7 he covered up and allowed Foreman to unload on him and he leaned on Foreman. Foreman's previous fights had mostly ended by the second round. He was the Mike Tyson of the early 1970's. Ali took everything Foreman had to throw at him and he wore him out and frustrated him.

At the beginning of the 8th round Ali saw in his eyes that Foreman was exhausted, frustrated, and that he was beat. And Ali took him out. There's a famous picture from ringside of Foreman on the mat and Ali looking over him. That's on my wall.

And to borrow a line from the great poet Marshall Mathers if and when the 8th round comes around for me, and I hope it does, "Best believe somebody's paying the pied piper" because someone is getting their ass kicked (sorry Mom—just to make a point. I know, I shouldn't have to use profanity to articulate my position).

I see faith as two huge mountains. On one side is us and on the other is God and eternal life. For some of us those mountains are very close and for others they are oceans apart. They ebb and flow through life as our faith journey ebbs and flows. They will never be flush—for faith is believing in something you can't prove with absolute certainty.

But my goal in life is to have them pretty darn close, so when the time comes for me to stand before God and give an account for my life it's a small step to make from this life to eternity.

And if per chance I am wrong? And if per chance all this religious stuff that we humans do is just hokus pokus and a way to make us feel better about our ultimate demise I will still say that living a life by following the teachings of Jesus Christ is a life well lived.

And I'd rather err on the side of safety for eternity's sake.

My opponents name is simply The Rumble. Ding Ding.

Round 1

When I find myself in times of trouble...

1st Song Out of Chemo
Dan Klein, February 6, 2014

There will be time for AC/DC & Journey later when the drugs really kick in.

For now, it's The Beatles. "Let it Be."

PS: my driver is really cute. :)

Let the Beatings Begin
By Claire Klein — February 6, 2014

It was nice to start our day with texts and posts from everyone showering us with their prayers and support. It has been a loooonnngggggg day here at Vandy. We checked in at 8:00 and had labs drawn. We then met with the nurse practioner, and headed to chemo 30 minutes early for our 10:00 appointment.

Our friend, Leslie, who has also gone through this, brought over a chemo prep bag last night. It has proven helpful, and we prayed one of her favorite novenas before starting the meds. Finally, at 12:20, the drugs were mixed and ready to be infused.

Prior to chemo starting, I was able to run around this place dropping breadcrumbs, so I could find my way back. I had to pick up some nausea meds, something to eat, and I had a little time to sit in the chapel. I continue to pray for healing, for those who are also stricken with illness, and as Dan always prays: those who have no one to pray for them.

The nurse is in here now pushing the last three drugs slowly through the IV. Only one of the four drugs infuses on its own. We didn't make our 1:00 consult with the radiology oncologist. We will try again next time.

Going to take this big guy home and tuck him in for a long winter's nap!

Note from Claire:
"I would not let him feel this loneliness."

We realized in this journey that our friends and family would carry us through to the finish line. About two weeks after our discovery of Dan's cancer, we decided it was time to tell our friends. That afternoon our couples' group and kids had an "Amazing Race" challenge all over Bowling Green followed by a pizza party. This was all planned by Dan and had been a good distraction for him that week. After the race, our friends—the Priests and Kunkels—who we had already told, kept the kids in the room with pizza, so that we could tell our other friends. It was such an emotional moment. As they waited for Dan to speak, no one would have imagined that this man, a picture of perfect health, would reveal that he had cancer. Suddenly as the information came forth, there was love. You could see it on their faces and feel it in their embraces. Faces of disbelief but friends who were willing to drop everything to help our family in need. This love that I truly felt was sent by God is what lifted us up and carried us through.

The following week, we got a second opinion at Vanderbilt in Nashville and felt at peace with our decision to undergo treatment there. Years ago, when we were starting our family, we experienced our own challenges of infertility. In the beginning stages, I found it to be one of the loneliest times of my life. I spent countless hours driving back and forth to Nashville mostly alone. Dan was very supportive but had to work and wasn't needed for the countless ultrasounds and blood tests. Now, with this new challenge, I would not let him feel this loneliness. I would be with him every step of the way. This was our journey together and we would travel the same road together. I would help him carry this cross. On days he couldn't, I would carry it for him.

Our family and friends became our support during this time. Our family kept us strong. My mom helped get the kids off to school when we left the house early for chemo. Dan's siblings visited on weekends to help with the kids and were a distraction for Dan when he was hurting from treatment. We found most of our support in our faith community. We were bombarded with meals and ice cream. One of our friends works for Smuckers and would bring us an overabundance of toppings. Every couple of weeks my supervisor made Dan his favorite peanut butter treats. We had donuts delivered by a Donut Fairy every Saturday morning. When Dan was down and out, our friends helped me get the boys to their practices. The hockey league offered to waive the three boys' fees. But most touching to me, they were willing to meet me at the gate and help get their gear on and skates laced. My least favorite task as a mother with three boys playing hockey. One of my friends took all of our linens and washed them. One of Dan's clients drove over from Glasgow weekly to mow our lawn. We received countless gift cards. One of them anonymous, gifting us a weekend at the Opryland hotel to relax once this terrible ordeal was over. And through it all, we realized this generous outpouring of love and support was beyond measure.

We often prayed for those who didn't have the support that we had. We became more aware of service to others. The real gift from these gestures was that our children realized that this is what you do when people are down and suffering. The best came out in people. We saw the best in people and hopefully it is a lesson that will stick with our children as they travel down their own paths in life.

Day One Wrap
By Dan Klein — February 6, 2014

Feeling good. Odd/bad taste in my mouth and a bit slug-gish/nauseous which was expected. For some odd reason the bottom of my feet hurt which I heard from someone else they experienced going through chemo. It makes you a bit nervous when the nurse puts on her HazMat suit to handle the syringe and then they pump it directly into your veins. Can't be good.

But all went well. Now we know what to expect from the logistical point of view. We shall see what comes to bear through the night. Having four kids, especially when we had a two year old who was and still is an early riser and premature twin babies who had to eat every 3-4 hours the whole up-all-night is not our favorite way to spend the night but we have some experience with it. Hopefully it will be a non-event.

Right on cue tonight the *Jesus Calling* devotion today hit the nail on the head for what we're dealing with. The title was "Rest."

"When you're so tired you can hardly stand, doesn't it feel wonderful when you finally get to sink into you own bed?...

Just as your body gets tired, so does your spirit...

Come to me. Lift up your hands in prayer to Me. Lie back and rest in My Presence. Take a deep breath of My Peace. I will refresh you and give you the strength to keep going."

One thing that has really started to sink in for me is that

when someone else is dealing with cancer or something else I am concerned for that person. But I can set it aside for awhile. I can shelf it. I can pick it back up when it's convenient or I think of it.

But when you are the one it is always weighing on you and leaning on you and you don't have the option to park it for a day or an hour or ten minutes. It's always there. And that's getting old and it's something I need to work on.

Still Standing
By Dan Klein — February 7, 2014

Not much rest, but that's ok. I know my body is off and I feel a bit like I've been punched in the stomach. Not cool. But I know I need to move forward because this will be the easiest round. Today I got the boys to school and rolled into work.

I am not turning my day over to chemotherapy.

Whatever your chemotherapy is for today work through it. Don't turn your day over to that.

What Do You Call. . .
By Dan Klein — February 9, 2014

So I'm lying in bed Friday night and it's around 10:15. Tired but feeling ok. I'm planning on going to Owensboro for the Catholic Men's Conference in the morning. The family has kind of adopted the man cave recovery room (MCRR) as the hang out place of the house.

Not the original idea but that's ok.

Sis fell asleep and Claire and the boys and I are all on the bed watching the opening ceremonies of the Olypmics. Hard to believe but it's been four years since we packed up the three boys and headed to Vancouver for the 2010 Winter Olympics. We love the Olympic spirit!

So I'm about to close my eyes for the night when all heck breaks loose. I hear something over my shoulder and into the MCRR rolls one of my old college buddies from St. Louis.

What is this!?!?! Then another, and another, until there are five of them right there. Shocked, indeed. But not surprised. I knew they would come. But I didn't expect them to come so soon.

Well played gentlemen and Claire.

But wait, it gets better. So I get out of bed and we hang out for awhile. The next morning they agree to go sledding with the kids despite not having any clothes for that (play cancer card here). So we're sledding and having a snowball fight and all of a sudden someone grabs my hat and I turn around and there are three more of them who flew in from Chicago!

Eight! Count them. My eight college buddies from St. Louis, Chicago, and Milwaukee with busy lives and families and flights to catch with busy careers dropped everything within a week to come spend the weekend with me after my first round of chemo. How cool is that?!?

One of our traditions for a get together is that we all go to breakfast together Sunday morning before we shove off to go our different ways. It was fantastic to be sitting at Cracker Barrel this morning eating breakfast with those guys.

So what do you call a weekend with your old buddies when you need them the most? The best medicine ever!

First Punch Landed
By Dan Klein — February 10, 2014

Sunday evening the effects from the chemo reared its ugly head and I got a glimpse of what the next 6-7 months will look like. It's not pretty and I'm aware round one is as easy as it's going to get.

That's humbling to say the least. Scary, if I'm totally honest.

Bad flu like symptoms and not able to get comfortable and not sure if I was hot or cold and really tired. Really tired. Put on top of that Natalie wanting to play duck-duck-goose in bed and it took a bit for it to pass. Thankfully it did pass or at least got better after a few hours and I was able to eat ice cream. FYI: the distress signal is when I can not eat ice cream.

I feel pretty lousy today but up and moving. Had a hard time reading the Proverbs chapter this morning which was a weird sensation. It seemed like the letters kept scrambling around the page. Just a reminder that this thing is indeed "on" and the poison is flowing. I am coming to this realization that the drugs and I have a quirky understanding. I agree to allow them to be pumped into my veins and they can do as much damage as they can and can make my life uncomfortable in exchange for getting rid of the cancer. We're on the same team but it's an uneasy alliance to say the least.

I felt pretty good about round 1 the first couple of days in. My college buddies I know had something to do with that. I did 3 laps at Keriakes yesterday, walking laps, because I could feel it coming on by mid-afternoon and figured I'd try to combat it by getting the blood flowing and heart pumping. I think next time I'll just take a Tylenol and head to bed.

Round 1—not knocked to the mat but first punch landed and felt. Eleven more to go. Easier said than done but one day at a time. It's easy to get overwhelmed to think about six months of this so I try not to. I told God again this morning I trust Him and wherever we are going with this I'm locked in.

It's not enough but thank you.

The Power of Accountability
By Dan Klein — February 11, 2014

I'm not a fan of New Years Resolutions. I think if there are things in your life you can and want to change that the calendar is an irrelevant marker. As soon as you identify something you want to improve you should take steps to do so—easier said than done, I know, and I'm as guilty as anyone.

And then there are some things you can't change and that's just the way the world works and that's ok. Life's not always fair as I am well aware.

I am, however, a believer in setting goals. Years ago I was

exposed to SMART goal setting and have implemented the SMART goal setting process. SMART stands for Specific, Measurable, Accountable, Reachable, Timeframe.

Rather than saying I'm going to get in better shape I will write down on paper and tell someone else about it using the SMART process—I am going to work out three times a week for the next three months and I want you to hold me accountable. Rather than say I am going to eat better I will write down I will eat three pieces of fruit a day for the next three months, etc, etc. Then I type up my little spreadsheet and put it somewhere that I can see it on an ongoing basis, currently the side of the fridge, and I put my little check marks in the box to track my progress every week.

I have a group of three friends and we serve as each others accountability partners. At the end of 2013 we got together and shared each of our personal, professional, and spiritual goals using the SMART format.

We allowed each other to poke holes and challenge our goals and make sure they were aligned with the SMART format and what we wanted to accomplished. We get together for lunch the first Tuesday of the month and using the SMART format we can very easily measure how we are doing. It's a powerful process and thankful to those guys for doing it.

I'm having a low key day getting things done around the house with all the kids spoken for. I start to feel a little better and I start to think about going to work out at D1 today. Sounds good in theory but not vey appealing. I talked myself into it and out of it several times and finally had myself talked out of it—its cold, im tired, i need my strength, on and on—but I know I need to do it. I know it would help.

So I text my three accountability partners and ask them to text me at 5:30 and ask me how boot camp went. Now I don't have a choice, dang it, and I have a date with 4:30 boot camp. I hit boot camp and worked out for an hour and actually felt pretty good. No records set, but felt good. It was good to break a sweat and get the muscles working and heart thumping again. I got the texts from them on schedule and reported back that I did it.

If it wasn't for that I dont think I would have held myself accountable to going. And who ever really feels like working out anyways? Thanks guys. I needed that big time.

I feel great tonight. Appetite is good. Almost back to pre-chemo status. Good night sleep would be welcomed. Thanks for the prayers and support. I feel them and use them. I got 7 1/2 days to enjoy before going back for round two next Wednesday.

Last Day of Round 1
By Dan Klein — February 18, 2014

We'll head back to Vandy for Round 2 in the morning. Assuming the cycle stays the same and the cumulative effects begin to pile up today will be as good as it is going to be. So I'm going to enjoy what I am guessing is the best I will feel for a long time. I feel pretty darn good—not great. But I would say everyone wakes up and has certain ailments to deal with. I managed through another boot-camp this afternoon. Not pretty but an hour of hard work felt good. Sleep is fair—better but not great. Thank you for the prayers on that and keep 'emcoming.

The constant punched-in-the-stomach feeling wore its welcome out pretty quick. It feels better if I take something for it but then the zombie feeling takes over and I'm not sure which one I prefer. So to this point it's been manageable. It's hard to eat when your stomach hurts but I keep trying to shovel it in. I'm not looking forward to that side effect gaining in magnitude.

I've attached my vision board to share. A vision board, not my original idea as most/all of what I do is not original, is a tangible picture of things you want to see happen. On one hand I look forward to the finish line but on the other hand I'm enjoying the first leg of the journey which I'm guessing will be the easiest. While it's important to take things one day at a time my inner-financial planner reminds me it is equally important to plan for the future.

My vision board has four pictures and it represents something that I want to make happen/look forward to seeing happen in July (end of chemo), August (end of radiation), September (getting strength back), and October (hopefully done with the whole darn thing!). I can look at my vision board and know time will pass and before I know it this whole thing will, hopefully, be behind me forever. It's a constant reminder of the big picture.

So starting clockwise in the top right is a picture of my Mom (Hi Mom!). And let me pause here and just simply say how blessed I am to have incredible parents. Thanks Mom & Dad. I love you. So Mom is standing at the end of the dock at my Uncle Earl and Aunt Sharon's cottage, otherwise known as the Hartman Family cottage at Higgins Lake in Northern Michigan. The spot where she is standing is my chemo finish line. Every 4th of July there is the Hartman Family reunion either there or at Aunt Marge and Uncle Doug's cottage across the lake. Mom & Dad rent the cottage from Uncle Earl and Aunt Sharon for three weeks afterwards and invite my siblings and me and our families to stick around or come back at our convenience. It's a very special time and it's worthy of a post all to itself.

Mom is standing watching the grandkids playing on the raft where she, as a teenager, played and learned to water ski—as did I when I was a kid, along with the rest of my brothers and sisters and cousins in our Hartman generation.

Beyond that, in what those belonging to the Hartman clan know as "the deep blue" because of how the color of the lake changes so drastically, is my sister Caroline in the front of the boat and I'm in the back getting someone ready to go for a tube ride.

I don't know or think I will make it this year because my last chemo treatment is scheduled for July 9th.When I get there, maybe next year, I will walk out to the end of that dock and get on my knees and look out over that beautiful piece of God's creation and thank Him for getting me through chemo, hopefully for good, and kiss that spot.

It's an ambitious goal to set for getting there this year and I love setting high goals, but I also believe in realistic goals. Thanks to Caroline and Mary, my two favorite sisters, for already offering to do whatever it takes to get me or at least the kids there. Thanks for looking out for your baby brother.

In the bottom right on my vision board is your classic first day of school picture representing August. Natalie was not so excited about it and despite Claire's best efforts to get one decent picture the best we got was the boys patiently smiling and posing while she is walking out of the frame. Instant Classic!

The bottom left is a picture from Mammoth Cave and is September. What an incredible natural treasure we have in our backyard—20 miles up the road. We rarely go in the caves, but we love hiking the trails and canoeing. And often times we'll grab some friends and go up mid-afternoon, go for a hike, and then build a fire and sit around cooking dinner and s'mores over the fire and watch the stars come out. And then pack up and in 30 minutes we're home in our own beds—which Claire really likes.

The last couple of years we have started canoeing every Memorial Day and Labor Day weekend and I'm looking forward to setting out on the river on Labor Day this year—chemo and radiation done!

The top left is October and is my mental finish line for the whole entire thing. That is the beach at WaterColor, Florida. It's our Fall Break destination again this year with our good friends the Yerics and George & Gail. The first thing I am going to do is get Natalie buckled into the seat behind me on my bike and peddle down to the beach, walk down that boardwalk and straight into the Gulf of Mexico holding her. That moment will come. It will be here. I can feel the cool water on my feet and the warmth of the sun on my face. I can feel the waves washing on my legs and a sense of completion as I write the last page of this chapter of my life called cancer—hopefully never to be opened again. It's only ten months away. I've lived a lot of ten month stretches in my life and they've all seemed pretty easy I suppose. I'll need to muster through this one.

I'm looking forward to breakfast with the guys at 6:00 tomorrow. Then we'll head for Nashville around 7:30. Meet with the radiologist, blood work, oncologist,and then head to chemo and finally home and wait for what I know is looming. Round 2.

Thank you again for all the love, support, prayers, and acts of kindness. Truly amazing and what a wonderful lesson to our children about the kindness that people are capable of and the character of the community we call home.

Proverbs Chapter 18:14

"One's spirit supports one when ill, but a broken spirit who can bear?"

Reflections From the End of the Dock: The Unknown

What are the right emotions to feel when you sit waiting for your first round of chemotherapy? Sitting in the chemo waiting room awaiting the dreaded poison. Most people are there in pairs—a patient and a caregiver. We are no different. Claire and I both have our reading and iPads. They are safely stashed away as we just sit. It's quiet. It's somber.

You become aware of the different patients. You can guess where they are in their treatment based on their appearance. Some are just sitting waiting patiently. Some are in wheelchairs with IVs standing next to them. My new peer group. Will that be me in six months?

It's a different energy than your typical doctor's office or hospital. There's almost a touch of serenity. Just a different perspective coming from the chemo waiting room compared to your typical waiting room. No one is concerned that they are running an hour or even two behind. No one keeps getting up to ask the lady at the desk where they are in line. It's almost a bit refreshing to have this unspoken acceptance. There's a void of the typical frustration or even agitation that you may normally get with a long wait. You want to get called but you don't. It's ok to wait.

Some of the patients, the ones with no hair, are obviously further along with treatment. In an odd way I am jealous of them. They know what to expect. I do not. In an odd way I am jealous of them because they have some time paid into their treatment cycle. I do not. I'm at the starting line.

I'm jealous of an old, bald, frail cancer patient sitting in a wheelchair. That's where I am right now. A month ago I was working out and playing basketball. I was getting on my son about dropping a hot dog. What a difference a month can make. Now I sit with a little buzzer in my hand waiting for it to light up and vibrate. The signal for me to enter the ring.

Finally, it buzzes. We grab our things and go to the desk and meet the nurse standing there. "Name and date of birth?" Trigger. We walk slowly back through the halls of the chemo ward—Infusion Center is its official name. Lots of small rooms line the hallways with nurse's stations at certain intervals.

Some curtains pulled shut. Others open. Some movement from the mix of patients, caregivers, and nurses but not much. We get situated in a room with two recliners and a curtain. Not very big but big enough.

I've already had the IV needled in my arm from my blood work this morning. It's held tight to my arm with purple stretch tape. The only sign at this stage that I am the patient.

It's an easy transition to take off that tape and plug in the tube from the IV stand. Knowing it's our first time, the nurse walks us through the process.

My chemotherapy is four different drugs. One of them, the largest in quantity, can be fed in by an IV drip. The others are "pushed" in because they are too thick to just drip in. We start with 20-30 minutes of fluid and then the poison drip begins. That usually takes a couple of hours. The bag that hangs at the top of the IV stand that is now connected to my arm by a long thin IV line is covered in this odd light green jacket. When we ask about it the nurse tells us that is to shield it from sunlight and she goes on to explain something about the chemical reaction if it gets too much sunlight. She then makes sure we have the pillows and heated blankets we need and tells us she'll check back in with us after a bit. Claire leans over and gives me a kiss and pats my back.

"Get some sleep. Your body needs it."

And so chemotherapy has begun. The nurse checks on us from time to time. After an hour or so someone in a blue volunteer vest politely enters and asks if we'd like any snacks. They wheel in a snack tray with a variety of snacks and drinks.

The nurse comes back and checks the IV bag. Satisfied it is empty she plucks it a couple of times with her finger and then says she'll be back with the others. She returns but this time she is in a suit that looks like something Homer Simpson wears at the nuclear plant.

She pulls up a chair and begins to switch over from the IV bag to her syringes. I'm a little unsure of this whole hazmat suit thing. She somewhat apologies for the get-up as she begins to push in the poison, slowly. I can see the veins in my arm, already aware that something isn't right, begin to define and almost bulge as they try to handle the thickness of the poison.

We begin to talk. When you are sitting less than two feet from someone for the better part of an hour it's hard not to talk. Claire and I enjoy and appreciate getting to know the different nurses and their stories over the coming months. It takes a special person to work at a cancer center and most people aren't just there for the paycheck. We appreciate that.

When the last drop of poison is done and a little additional fluid pumped in to help circulate I finally get unplugged. After the better part of four hours the IV comes out. I slowly stand up. The headache is already setting in.

We gather our belongings. I put on my backpack and slowly follow Claire down the hall and to the elevator. We get to the valet parking and Claire gives them our ticket. The car quickly pulls up and they help me in. We offer the valet attendant a $5 bill and he politely but firmly refuses and ask that we put it in the church collection this Sunday.

I get settled in the front seat. We exchange a "here we go" kind of look and slowly begin to move away from Vanderbilt. Heading home. Heading to life with chemo. I know this isn't going to go well. I recognize this as a necessary step in the process and there's no way to get out of it. It's coming. Knowing it is coming but not knowing exactly what "it" is only makes things worse.

I begin to go through my iTunes songs. An act that would become a symbolic part of our routine. Looking for the right song to play. The appropriate song for that leg of the journey to capture the emotion of that exact moment.

...Let it be

Round 2

Country road, take me home...

1st Song Out of Chemo
By Dan Klein — February 19, 2014

John Denver. "Take Me Home, Country Roads."

Very long day but finally homeward bound.

Round 2
By Dan Klein — February 20, 2014

Let me throw this disclaimer out there and I'll probably do it more times than once. I'm very uncomfortable with opening this window to our lives. We tend to be more private with our family and our faith, as I mentioned in the "My Story" portion. Some who read this who have known me for a long time—or even a short time—may be a bit taken aback by my faith.

I guess I didn't do a good enough job living out my faith when I was around you and I would amend a popular phrase to "there are no atheist in fox holes or oncology waiting rooms."

Being told you have cancer seems to grant you a little deeper perspective with this whole God thing.

Opening up like this is very awkward for me and I'm not sure if it is helpful to me. And I reserve the right at anytime without warning to give you the boot and shut it down.

But as I have said here and at the Annointing, God is

leaning on me and I'm learning that this whole thing is more about you and less about me. And for anyone who believes God has laid something in their heart to do and they try to ignore it or make excuses for not doing it, well, you are asking for trouble.

The worst possible downside of the fear of failure for trying something—in this case, opening up this uncomfortable window—and if it goes horrifically wrong and you do indeed fail, just remember that the cost is nominal compared to the feeling of regret of not trying at all.

So Round 2 has not been kind to me and I have met the mat. It was a head shot and not a body shot. The meeting with the radiologist yesterday didn't land very softly with me. We liked and appreciated his honesty and no sugar coating approach. And I think/hope he is doing what I would do if I were in his shoes and call it like it is and say maybe things get better with this but as of right now we have some issues.

It's just a reminder that despite Hodgkin's being very treatable and curable this thing is extremely serious both for this year and the rest of my life. I'm more of a math guy than a medical guy and I can run the numbers on probability of this side-effect and that side-effect and the list—both short term and long term—is substantial. Then the whole % chance of the treatment that is used to cure this cancer jacks up my probability to be hit with another cancer down the road. Crap.

The last point stuck with me. Even if that probability is only 5-10% a year, my math says that is once every 15 years. The way I figured it, and yes my logic may have flaws, if I live to be 80, and yes I am indeed a half full kind of guy, I will endure 2-3 additional bouts with cancer and they won't be as "friendly" as Hodgkin's and it will be my ultimate demise—I don't really want to go out that way; going through treatment after treatment only to come to the point where I eventually decide not to take any more. Be it 18 months or 40 years from now.

And, of course, it may never come back. But that whole thing impedes your sleep a bit—or at least mine.

So I let The Rumble get the better of me last night. I've been up since 1:30 wrestling with it but after trying to shut it off and praying for rest I finally gave in and just got out of bed. The first thing waiting for me was the usual spot on text and words of encouragement and experience from Leslie & Cravens. Perfect.

Then I read my Proverbs: 20:18 "Plans made with advice succeed; with wise direction wage your war." & 20:24 "Our steps are from the Lord; how, then, can mortals understand their way?" Perfect.

Then I sat in silence for a bit which is always a premium around my house. Perfect.

Then I read the first four chapters of the gospel of Matthew. One of the guys from breakfast shared a schedule to spend five minutes a day for reading the New Testament in a year. So, tired, I started reading. I got to chapter four and felt like God had just been waiting for me and was probably a little pissed off it took me that long to get there since, after all, He has other things to do today, you know.

It reminded me of the saying "When the student is ready the teacher will arrive." Chapter four is about when the devil tried to tempt Jesus. After Jesus resisted him "Then the devil left him and, behold, angels came and ministered to him." Man was that what I needed—if Jesus Christ, son of God who could walk on water and do other really cool things (imagine bringing that guy to a party), could get knocked down and need to be ministered to, surely lowly me with all my many weaknesses and imperfections can allow myself to get knocked down as well.

So I texted Mike and thanked him for ministering to me even though he had no idea—that's the funny thing about living your life through Proverbs I think you minister to people through the way you live without even knowing about it. Perfectly perfect.

Have an awesome day. I know I will (a good nap being part of that). And I'll try my best and lean on God to not allow me to turn this day over to chemotherapy.

Back on my feet! What's your chemotherapy today? Work through it.

Knocked Down
By Claire Klein — February 22, 2014

A quick journal for those of you missing your Dan time. He has been hit harder with this second round. I knew he was feeling rough, when he skipped his ice cream last night. He has been in bed most of the day but rallied for his bowl of ice cream tonight!

Hopefully, things are looking up.

We moved devotion time upstairs to the man cave. Dan was most thankful that this day is almost over and we can start anew tomorrow.

Note from Claire

I journaled the first year of our relationship. I was a college sophomore and Dan a freshman. He had a girlfriend back home when we first met. We were drawn to each other. Over the semester and a half, we became close. Too close for that high school relationship to last. I had a persistent roommate who insisted just before Christmas break that we lie under that huge Christmas tree in the quad to wish on a star. That night, in freezing temperatures, there was only one star in the sky. I wished on that one star. I wished for Dan Klein.

Once we officially became a couple, it was always easy. Dan is an easy going guy. He is loyal and when he loves, he loves strong. We love strong. Our family is an indication of this. We took our vows to heart on June 22, 1996. I promise to be true to you in good times and in bad, in sickness and in health. I will love and honor you all the days of my life. Oh boy, did we have good times. We had good jobs, traveled, started a family, and spent quality time with our extended families.

I always had that thought in the back of my mind that life was too good. We had our health. I remember going to the Outer Banks in the summers for a week. We would meet my mom's best friend and her family from New York. I would stand at the water's edge, listening to the waves crash, and looking out at the Atlantic Ocean. I would wish that we could freeze time at that very moment. Everyone important to me was healthy. We had so many good times and no bad times to speak of.

We learn that if we take that leap and risk loving, we also risk losing. That's the hard part. We don't think about this when we meet the boy of our dreams. We only envision the good times and put the bad times aside.

So, it is in sickness and in health, that might be the real

challenge. When you love someone, you persevere. You maintain that purpose in spite of difficulty. You love and honor that special person all the days of your lives.

Back to the land of the living
By Dan Klein — February 23, 2014

It's nice to be vertical again. I made a couple of attempts yesterday to get moving and it just wasn't happening. Around 5:30 yesterday afternoon I got out of bed for about an hour. Enough time to grab a blanket and sit out on the deck and see the sun shine for a bit.

If I've ever felt that lousy before I certainly don't remember it.

I felt it coming on Friday night right on cue and then after about 36 hours I can feel it gradually ratchet down the intensity level as I do right now. Thank you Lord! Thankfully no nausea symptoms but oh, the aches and the shakes. The freezing feet and hands and hot restless legs.

Sleep is still a mess. I just try to get it where and when I can. I'll plan on sleeping in September. Nurse Claire and Nurse Natalie are taking good care of me. Although Natalie prefers to be known as a waitress.

My first goal for today is to walk down to the mailbox by 1:00. That's about 200 yards away and surely I can do that. If that's no problem I may try to do a lap on the trail at Kereiakes later today. That may be a bit ambitious but I have to get the blood flowing.

It's amazing how swiftly the poison takes over and then that sweet, sweet feeling of knowing it is finally subsiding. It goes without saying I have a new profound respect for people who have gone through this.

Two down and I'm not thinking about #3 yet. I'm just going to enjoy the next 9 days. I'm a long way from feeling good or even average and that's just how things are going to be for awhile and that's ok. This too shall pass.

Round 2 lingering
By Dan Klein — February 25, 2014

I'm not a fan of complaining because I'm not sure what good comes from it especially if its not changing anything. But sometimes it just feels good to gripe about something and get it out of your system and then you move on.

So the cycle seems to have the big drop and then the big recovery followed by smaller drops and smaller recoveries—kind of like a roller coaster. And while some characteristics are consistent I can say through two rounds, each round is unique in its own way. I did get a block of sleep last night of around five hours thanks to a little prescription sleep aid.

That's the longest block of sleep I've had since this baby has started. Can't say I feel great but it's good to get a chunk of sleep.

And I'm going to bitch (sorry Mom) about my mouth. My teeth hurt. What the heck is that?? And I went to floss the other night and started with my back teeth and the first thing I did was carve out a little chunk of gum. Ouch!

So my gums are a little soft these days. Better believe I'm darn careful with flossing. And now entering the ring is a side effect that I am going to predict will be one my least favorite when it is all said and done—open sores in my mouth and throat. Dang these babies hurt. Every swallow

I imagine the little chemo gremlin's call light goes on, signaling to it to stab my throat or roof of my mouth. They set down the little book they were reading or their cup of coffee, grab their rusty fork, and shove it as hard as they can into their assigned spot and give it a good twist.

In talking with others who have gone through chemo they were not fond of these suckers either. I counted about a dozen—roof of my mouth, corners, back of throat. Talk about making eating more difficult.

So there's my complaint of the day. There's not a lot I can do about any of those so I'm handing, more like shoving, those off to God and asking very nicely for Him to take it. I'm just very thankful there's an end to this journey, hopefully, and I have incredible compassion and my heart hurts for people who go through this without having a good prognosis. It's one thing to know and hope it's temporary. I can't begin to fathom this becoming more or less a lifestyle. That would break me in a heartbeat.

I almost didn't do ice cream last night but it was an act of defiance on my part so I had a small amount. I imagined those little crappy gremlins in my throat shivering as the ice cream came down. Bastards. The logistical help with the kids is incredibly helpful to Claire—which means you will forever be in my favor.

Today is a new day and I am just focusing on what God wants me to do. That's no different from my pre-cancer life. The flood waters eventually recede. The sun does indeed rise on a new day. Today is not dress rehearsal for life. It is life. What you and I choose to do with this day has a cost. That cost is one day of our life that we will never get back. Let's both make it count.

Strong Weekend

By Dan Klein — March 1, 2014

This weekend is my strong weekend and I'm trying to take advantage of it. Wednesday begins my fight week as round 3 begins. Not looking forward to next Friday night when the poison starts throwing haymakers.

I made it to Mammoth Cave Friday morning with my good friend, Joe Kunkel. It was 23 degrees and as I pulled up Joe said he thought chemo just messed up my body and not my head.

Thanks again Joe, let's do it again sometime.

I'm afraid my days of boot camp and trail hiking are numbered. I'm a firm believer in mental and spiritual health beginning with the body so I may have to find a pool somewhere to get my work outs in. I owe my accountability partners three workouts a week and I can't let them down so I'm going to have to figure something out fast. And next Tuesday is our accountability day for the month and you guys better be ready. We're going to see the movie "Lone Survivor" and I'm really looking forward to that time.

My main gripe, and really only other one today—thank you Lord for relief from those dang mouth sores—is my right forearm hurts pretty bad and the pain extends up if I over use it—like in typing. That's the risk of getting chemo via IV versus a port. The veins in your arm can get horribly messed up and eventually you can have hardening of the veins. I don't need anything else at this point physically to go downhill so I'm going to get the port put in my chest Tuesday.

Sleep is getting better but is still hit or miss—mostly miss. Ok almost always a miss.

So if you're thinking about working out or going for a walk but just don't "feel like it"—as I say to my accountability partners: don't let the guy with cancer taking chemo beat you.

I've had someone say this to me and have read that people who have cancer get this "gift." I'm still getting my hands around it to be able to articulate it but I think it's the gift of having life in focus. Like NASA high zoom focus. You just get what's important and what's not to the nth degree.

It's one thing to hear something and still another to believe something. And yet still another to live it. There are things that I've thought I'd like to do at some point in my life and have figured out I just need to chart my path and go. If it, not I, fails that's ok. And if nothing else it's a good life lesson to my kids. Better to have tried and failed than to not try at all.

As the great poet Garth Brooks once wrote—"Life is not tried, it is merely survived if you are standing outside the fire." Bring on the heat baby.

The Hair Thing
By Dan Klein — March 3, 2014

I come from a family where the men do not have a very good track record with hair. That may be an understatement. I think my Dad and brothers are probably snickering a bit at this whole hair thing and that finally I get to join the bald club. I will point out it is a temporary membership gentlemen—although I've been told it can come back a different color and texture.

I have put in the request for a red afro. I think that will go well with a tall skinny guy and it can only increase my chance of getting cast on "Survivor" or "Amazing Race." Much like the albino elephant draws a crowd at the zoo.

"What's up with that tall, skinny, red afro guy who says his "O's" like he's from Michigan yet still draws out his "E's" like a southerner???"

So I got that going for me.

I feel darn near outstanding today. Hit the wall early afternoon and had to shut it down for a couple of hours. Thanks Claire and Mrs. Hensley for taking care of the kids today. All day. I really am not looking forward to starting round three but that's still one and a half days away so I'm going to enjoy the next 36 hours of my strong week.

The hair thing—it is going slowly and steady. We're probably days from needing to get the clippers out and have me join the other Klein men in the club. But laughter is good medicine and I was getting ready for church Sunday I thought of something my Dad said: As you get older you get hair where you dont want it and lose it where you want it.

When I was in high school I got an earring much to my parent's dismay. And that fad lasted a year or so and out it came—actually the day I met Claire's parents for the first time. On my ear there's a small spot/scar from that. Let's just say the piercing wasn't a professional grade job to begin with.

As I got older Mother Nature, in her infinite wisdom, has seen fit to allow a single dark hair grow from that spot thus fulfilling my Dad's prophecy.

So when I think of it or Claire points it out I clip it. No big deal. But Sunday I was getting ready for church about ready to clip it and leaned into the mirror and thought, nope, Im going to keep that sucker.

Reflections From the End of the Dock:
The Finish Line of Comfort

The first few days of this round were definitely a tender spot in the early journey. A gut check. A point of critical mass for exhaustion and frustration. It came out in the first few paragraphs of my journal entry "Round 2." Nobody questioned my faith. Except maybe me. Nobody made negative comments. Except maybe me. The underlying stress just came out. Fatigue took over.

Sometimes when there's something bothering you, for whatever reason, that stress expresses itself towards other people or things that have nothing to do with the original source. I think parenting can be a lot like that. A stressful situation at work and suddenly I'm not the caring and loving husband and father I try to be but the tired, distracted, and impatient husband and father. I've come to appreciate through cancer that in life it's easy to do things when everything is going your way. It's easy to smile and approach and even attack life with meaning and purpose when everything is falling into place nicely. Anyone can deliver in ideal circumstances. But when a tailwind becomes a headwind that's when it really counts. That's the difference. And the first part is being able to recognize the situation for what it is. "Damn, this is hard and I am not at my best but I have to push through this." This is where the growth begins.

Even though radiation is still five months away—an absolute eternity in chemo time—it's part of the process of treatment to begin getting familiar with the radiation oncologist and for whatever testing and levels they need to start monitoring. To this point in treatment it's just been day to day. Just get through today. Check it off. We are meeting with the radiologist. He's very knowledgeable, or confident, or both. We like him but he's no David and Leslie. He pulls up the scan and begins to talk about the "field". Where they are going to be targeting the radiation. He points out the biggest part of the mass which is "a safe distance from your vital organs." Then points out this smaller part close to the lungs and then there's this one little spot by the heart "which really concerns me."

I knew Mom was following CB. There were certain things I didn't include specifically to keep her from knowing about them. This was one of them.

"If chemo doesn't get it I'm sure we can, but that's putting a lot of radiation close to your vital organs."

Then, more matter-of-fact than I cared for, he begins. He begins to rattle off the potential side effects. And on and on he went. The slow and steady barrage was more than I had prepared for and wanted to hear. More than I could hear. There's a reason why we don't always tell people what they really want to or need to hear. It's just not fun being the bearer of bad news.

But at the cancer center sugar coating isn't an option.

I'm sitting on yet another darn exam table and swallowing hard and working really hard at keeping my emotions in check. And on he goes. Overwhelming to a guy doing everything he can to get through the next several days. It's a cruel irony for a young cancer patient. The same "medicine" they use to heal you this go around, may very well be what brings you back and what ultimately kills you in the end.

That's too much of a load in a fragile state. I'm dreading just getting through the next seven days. How do I begin to grasp that all of this could be the first in a series of bouts with The Rumble? What the heck is the point? Good Lord, I need you.

There's a place on the trail that I like to walk at a nearby park—Kereiakes Park—where I came to see it for what it was. The finish line of comfort. If you walk it casually you'll probably never notice it. But when you walk it over and over and over again the subtleties of the trail stick out. There are stretches that allow for brief relief with a good downward slope. As well as stretches that are more demanding, like a steep uphill climb. When you find yourself on that trail all times of the day and night—be it 3:00 AM or 3:00 PM—you get very familiar with it. You notice things the casual walker or runner may miss. Add on top that you feel absolutely horrible before you even take your first step and the subtleties suddenly begin to scream out.

On the very back of the trail there's a good size hill. You go down and then back up. That's ok. But when you reach the bottom and see the short intense upward climb back up you know what you're up against. You can prepare. You can muster through it. I can get through one round of chemo.

It's when you get to the top of that hill and the trail makes a 90 degree turn to the right. It's 100 yards of a very slight incline. Your body feels it more so than your mind sees it.

It doesn't recognize it for as much of a challenge as it is. Therefore you don't adequately prepare. You just feel more resistance and more fatigue than your mind assumes. But a lifetime of side effects or relapses?

The big climbs—a biopsy or round of chemo—you know it's coming and you can prepare. But it's the little things that lean in on you. The cumulative effects of those slight and steady inclines. That slight headwind combined with the mental disconnect of the effort required. That leads to the finish line of comfort. There you can find fatigue accompanied by frustration. There it's easy to shut it down because there's seemingly no explanation for those emotions. Just exhaustion.

But when I was able to recognize that point—a long slight incline I didn't really see following a steep hill that I most definitely saw and most definitely prepared for—I came to appreciate something. In life it's not always the big events that pose the most difficult struggles. Not everyone will be faced with a cancer diagnosis or some other steep hill that, while traumatic, allows you to recognize it for what it is and adequately prepare. But those slight but steady headwinds we all face. Those slight but steady ones that don't necessarily register but constantly push and bring us to that point of exhaustion. And from that point, the point of exhaustion, is where progress can be made.

It's not the entire 60 minutes of boot camp that allows growth. It's dumping everything you got and working hard the first 50 minutes to get yourself to the point of muscle exhaustion and mental frustration. Muscles, tired and sore. Lungs and heart thumping. The last ten, when you're beyond your comfort zone, you move forward. You grow.

I've come to the awareness through cancer that the finish line of comfort and the starting line of growth look an awful lot alike.

…. to the place I belong

Round 3

**Took my love and I took it down.
Climbed a mountain and I turned around
and I saw my reflection in the snow
covered hills till the landslide
brought me down....**

1st Song Out of Chemo
By Dan Klein — March 5, 2014

"Landslide" by Fleetwood Mac.

Another long day but one step closer. Special thanks to my good friend Nick Noble for giving up his day and taking me down and being my wingman.

No port yet. That was moved to next week. I had an outstanding day yesterday. Thanks to Claire (she rocks; always has), Aunt Claire for making the trip, my accountability buddies for a great meeting followed by four guys going to see "Lone Survivor," and capped off by celebrating Fat Tuesday at Chuys with friends.

Started today right with proverbs and time in the classroom of silence. Then got the van out of the garage and—because of some snow and ice—slid into the backyard and got it stuck around 5:45. Jumped into my little Toyota to get to breakfast with our men's group for prayer and good discussion. Going to take more than one stuck van to keep me from that!

Headed out of breakfast around 7:30 to get the van out of the yard, kissed the wife and kids goodbye and headed out for Round 3.

Ding Ding. Here we go.

Very cool last 24 hours.

Next 24+ probably not so cool. Although I got about 48 hours before the punches start flying. Don't like missing mass on Ash Wednesday but thanks to Krista. She and the rest of the Yerics are joining us for devotion & ice cream tonight and she will make sure I get my ashes.

We have entered the grind. The initial adrenaline and shock have worn off and we're adapting to our new lifestyle with our unwanted and uninvited houseguest. An absolute daily grind.

Stuck in rush hour traffic in Nashville but slowly and steadily making our way—in more sense than one.

Round 3 Adjustments
By Dan Klein — March 6, 2014

I had an outstanding day. The best I have felt since January 12th I would venture to say (the 12th is the day *before* I found out I had cancer). I did get a decent night's sleep last night at least for me, 10:30-4:45. Not bad and it was a solid sleep.

I'm trying something new for Round 3 and making an adjustment. I'm going on the offensive. I ducked and covered for Round 2 and got my rear handed to me. So I'm coming out swinging this round. Doc thinks I may have just picked up a bug since my white blood count had pretty much bottomed out. Which seemed odd and awfully coincidental that the same time the chemo starts to hit I get a bug. But maybe so. Claire suggested since I got the flu shot with my chemo last time it may have been a reaction to the flu shot.

Makes more sense—and she doesn't have a degree from Yale and Stanford! That's my girl.

Hoping that's the case and this round is a little easier. Part of chemotherapy is they give you steroids along with the poison to help offset the effects at least for the first 24-48 hours. So I figured while I got the steroids pumping I might as well do what I can and not just curl up in a ball and suck my thumb and wait for the effects to crawl in.

Number one was a mental adjustment. I'm thinking of myself as just my usual self—not the guy with cancer. That may seem easy but I can honestly say not a minute—maybe two if I stretch—has gone by since January 13th where I am not aware of or actively thinking about the cancer that resides in my chest. I usually have some physical symptom that is kind enough to serve as that constant reminder. That gets old and weighs on you.

Water, with enough time, carved out the Grand Canyon. It doesnt have to be that strong, just constant. That line of thinking is natural and normal but it leans on you. So I made the conscious decision today to be just me. Not me who is dealing with cancer. Just me.

So I got in my morning prayers (Proverbs 6:9-10: "How long, O sluggard, will you lie there? when will you rise from your sleep? A little sleep, a little slumber, a little folding of the arms to rest—then poverty will come upon you like a robber, and want like a brigand."). Sounds like I need to get moving.

So I ate breakfast #1 (try to eat one when I get up and one later), and hit 6:00 AM boot camp this morning—not pretty but effective. And the only people crazy enough to do boot camp at 6:00 AM are serious—and that didnt help me from a comparison perspective. But it helped me to push harder. Felt good to last the entire hour.

There were times when I began to think of myself as the guy with cancer who had every reason and right to walk off that field. But I kindly dismissed that thought between huffing and puffing and made it through. I was proud of myself for making it through.

I also weighed in this morning pretty much at my normal morning weight since this began. Which is good. I don't need to lose weight. Those who are offering to lose weight for me? My Mom said she has first dibs.

The cycle has been this: I lose 5-7 pounds in the 48-72 hours during bad chemo time. Then work on putting it back on. Need a diet idea?

Full day at work, which was excellent and felt great—I'm blessed to have a job that I love and an outstanding team that I have the privileged to work with in Jodi and Jeremiah. And I have the best clients a financial planner could ever ask for. Truly blessed in that I get to do work that I am passionate about.

Signing off. Got to hit boot camp tomorrow one more time to throw one more punch before they start flying my way. Time for ice cream and sleep.

Good night, Dan—just Dan.

Quick Round 3 Update
By Dan Klein — March 8, 2014

Feeling much, much better this round. Earlier I emailed someone and said I feel like a rock star compared to Round 2, but it's probably more like a rock star the day after the concert. Either way, it's much better than not being able to physically get out bed. I did not do ice cream last night but plan on it tonight.

Thanks for all the prayers, good vibes, and support. They work.

Port is scheduled for next Tuesday here in BG. My Mom took me to pre-op today, always nice to have your Mom with you when you're not feeling well regardless of how old you are, and we made sure we stopped by the Donut Shop before hitting the MedCenter. :)

In addition to Mom and Dad stopping in on their way north from snowbirding, my sister and her family came south and are in town from Chicago. So all the kids have had a blast with their cousins and aunt and uncle and grand-parents at the Holiday Inn swimming and doing whatever they've been doing. House has been very quiet—very un-usual for the Klein house.

Needless to say I come from a very special family. Thanks Mom & Dad and Caroline & Mark.

Heading back to bed. Have a good weekend.

Ports in
By Dan Klein — March 11, 2014

All went well. Feels like a bottle cap is under my skin on my left chest. Not ideal but ok and with a little help from my chemical friend it feels fine.

Won't help the sleep situation I'm sure but that's ok. But as the *Jesus Calling* devotion reminded me tonight I don't have to rely on my own strength—thank you Lord. That's more significant than I can articulate because my tank ran out awhile back.

Tomorrorw starts my strong week and I'm ready! Round 3 was much much better than round 2. Much, much better. Thanks for prayers, love, support and special visit from the Dillons and Mom & Dad. Gives me a better outlook on rounds 4-12.

And the cards and food and random acts of kindness. It is a very humbling experience to witness your kindness. It's not even close to adequate but thank you. But more than anything thank you for supporting Claire and the kids.

I was craving cookie dough ice cream tonight and asked Claire to pick some up when she swung by Walgreens to get my chemical play buddy and told her to get whatever kind. Doesn't matter. Just cookie dough. Wouldn't you know she went to another place as well and got Ben & Jerry's.

That's my girl. You ask for something and she gives you something plus. Well done George & Gail. Hoping to feel well enough to make it to Diddle tomorrow night to cheer on the Lady Scotties. It's a later game and I turn into a pumpkin early but for the chance to see the Scotties in the KY Sweet 16, and hopefully some of my Glasgow friends, I'll just to need to ask God for that extra bit of energy.

Random factoid you didn't know about Scottie athletics and my wife: the 1990 "most athletic female" was the one and only Claire Katchak. She was also one of the first female athlete to break the gender barrier and play for the boys soccer team in addition to her superb basketball and softball play. I've seen the video. Impressive play and cute shorts. Wonder if we still have those...

And another impressive Claire Klein feat, while we're at it. All of you in Biliken nation already know that Claire was the Saint Louis University homecoming queen in 1994. Athletic, smart, beautiful, everyone's friend. How the heck did I land that??

As Natalie said to me the other day "crazy weird."

Many of you may know Claire as an incredible friend and mother and physical therapist. And she is all that and a bag of chips and so much more. We were known in college as "the happy couple" and since we met on that fateful bus trip that's been spot on.

It's tough living with someone that darn good. But it's freaking awesome!

Uh-oh—I just asked her to find some cologne I can put on to trump this nasty surgical cleansing smell that, dang it all, survived the shower. She found some but said it has cough medicine all over it. Shows how often I wear cologne—I think it was the Bush administration but not sure which one.

So lucky Claire gets to sleep with a guy with a horrible blend of surgical cleanser, Obsession, and NyQuil. Sweet!

I'll just be enjoying my time with my new chemical friend.

Quick Sunday Evening Post
By Dan Klein — March 16, 2014

We just finished our *Jesus Calling* and the kids are on their way up. Just a quick update. Round 3 Fight Week was much better but Round 3 Strong Week was tough. I'm still navigating my way through when to push and when to pull back and my body is pretty clear at letting me know when I have stepped outside the body's desired limits in a multitude of ways.

I am glad to have a reprieve from the constant headache and brain-freeze-feeling of chemo off the list of symptoms that's for darn sure. I have another couple of days to enjoy that. This week goes by so fast and I'm already knocking on another trip to Vandy. Ugh.

I'm also starting to experience insurancelitis—what insurance will cover and what it won't. That's a stack of paperwork and process I'm not really up for right now but it's a logistical necessity and its part of the grind. We're scheduled for a test on April 2nd which is a pretty important check in and I was notified the other day insurance will not cover it, so I need to put that on my list of to-do's.

It's just part of the grind. I think the hardest part of this whole thing is still that I can't set it down and forget about it for a couple of days or even a couple of hours and come back to it when its convenient or when I think of it. 24/7. Cancer is on.

I'm afraid my days of boot camp may be put on hold for the duration. Right foot still hurts—why the heck does my right foot hurt?? Mouth sores are better thankfully. I would equate it somewhat to having children. When we had one it seemed like all we could do to take care of that one. When we went from one to three it seemed three was all we could do and when we went from three to four . . you get the picture. But going the other way when someone is taken out of the mix— when you go from four to three (Yeah for Space Camp!) or four to one it's all of a sudden a piece of cake.

One of my favorite parenting quotes came from someone who had quads. They said, "we wonder what people who only have one child do with all their time, money, and sleep?"

So when you go from a dozen sores in your mouth to one stubborn sore it's a walk in the park and you pretty much forget it's even there until it cries or needs something. But it's taking me longer to do things these days which is frustrating. Longer to walk down the stairs. Longer to get my shoes on. Longer to concentrate and think through something. Longer to write. It's frustrating that being able to do daily things (ADLs to our PT/OT friends), and to even express yourself is being compromised.

Sometimes I feel like I can't even tie my gum and chew my shoes at the same time. Very frustrating.

So, all in all, I'd call Round 3 a draw. Fight week was good—I was never out of the fight. Strong week was not so good—I took the fight to the enemy but spread myself a little too thin. Still learning.

Still navigating. Still taking it one day at a time and trusting in God's strength to see me through.

Gearing up for Round 4
By Dan Klein — March 18, 2014

Getting ready to go and check another one off the list. Took it a bit easier today which was good. Nice as always to have Aunt Claire (Gail's sister) stay with us for a few days during treatment week.

I'm ready for the Rumble. I'm ready for Round 4. I'm just going to say I'm looking forward to it. Ok, maybe a stretch.

It is nice to match up chemo treatment with the first weekend of March Madness.

Feeling good today. A bit "off" but overall good. Everyone wakes up with something not working right so being a bit off is to be expected. Hair is hanging in there. Trying to avoid fans and strong winds. Getting a bit patchy, I must say. I'd prefer to keep it, but it is what it is.

At the cancer center a bald head is like your red badge of courage. Coming back from battle. You've been on multiple deployments. You're not the new guy heading in for the first time. You know someone who is bald is at least a good deal through their treatments. They are the veterans. The ones that walk a little slower but you are, in an odd way, happy for them because they got to be getting close to the end of their treatment and ultimately, hopefully being cured of this dreaded disease.

Closer than us hairies anyways. We rookie, hairy folk, still have the bulk of our treatment ahead of us. We walk a little quicker. We can even make it to the cafeteria for lunch if we really wanted. And when people look at us casually they really can't tell anything is wrong. I'll miss that much more than the hair.

So as the hair goes I shift from one peer group to another. Not this round, but I have a feeling next time, I will get the slight head nod from the baldies as they welcome me to their platoon. And I will look at the hairies with a bit more compassion knowing they are in the early stages of their treatment.

Through this ordeal, specifically the biopsies, I know what your mind tells your body matters. There's a reason I'm not in the medical field. Blood/needles/etc. can make me a bit queezy. Not convenient if you're the guy going through medical procedures on a regular basis, but I suppose you can get used to about anything.

After the first biopsy I figured if your mind can work against your body in a negative way, like making you pass out, it should stand to reason you should be able to tap into that power in a positive way. Can't say I've had a medical breakthrough in unlocking that secret, but I'm certainly working on it.

Proverbs 18:10:

"The name of the Lord is a strong tower; the just run to it and are safe."

Ding, Ding. Bring it on!

Reflections From the End of the Dock:
The Trail

*"Better a little with fear of the Lord
than a great fortune with anxiety."*
Proverbs 15:16

Kereiakes Park is a city park about ½ mile from our home that is next to a large cemetery. It's two baseball fields are where our boys play little league and we've spent countless late summer evenings coaching and cheering them on. About a dozen well kept and well lit tennis courts are where Claire meets her tennis buddies on a regular basis. As you turn into the main entrance from the street, Cemetery Road no less, there is a basketball court. Finally, there snakes a great Frisbee golf course through the trees on the back half of the park just beyond the large community garden.

Then there's the trail. It's a gravel path about ten feet wide and loops 1.25 miles around the outside of the park. It brings you past the tennis courts and baseball fields on the front end and then through the back half of the park with the old trees and hills.

That trail was my emotional outlet. On the back half of that path, far away from everything else and especially the kids, was where I tried to process all the emotions and terrible thoughts that cancer brings. It's where, when no one else was around, I would do my crying. As carefully as I could, I sifted through the tender spots and tried the best I could to do a control release of all that raw emotion that comes with being a father of young children and husband going through cancer.

So many unfair thoughts and conversations I had with myself as I walked through the old trees. The trees that I suddenly became jealous of as I came to realize they have been here long before me and will be here long after me. I remember one time seeing a leaf fall from its branch. I stopped on the trail and watched. It twirled and circled until it gracefully came to rest on the ground directly in front of me. Aware that it was early summer, the prime time of the year, and much too early for a leaf to fall. Aware that my life, too, was in early summer.

I saw it as a metaphor for life. A life, just like a leaf on the tip of a branch, goes through the natural life cycles and experiences the seasons. Ultimately attached delicately to a branch that has provided everything for it and supported it. The branch is attached and part of a larger structure of the trunk fed by roots that run for centuries. All of the history. All of the energy and life pushing forward yet so reliant on the past. All meant for one beautiful and dazzling day in autumn.

Some fall earlier in the season than others. Some hold

on to the very end and slowly fall. Some are violently shaken from their branch early. Just one strong wind away—one diagnosis away—from being released and falling to the ground.

Sometimes that leaf becomes part of a larger group of leaves that fly fantastically on the wind surrounded by other leaves. It creates a beautiful scene of nature. A vibrant life that impacts all those who witness it. Other times, a single leaf falls, unnoticed, somewhere in the forest.

When it does come to settle on the ground that leaf eventually breaks down. It goes back into the ground. Ashes to ashes. Dust to dust. It provides whatever small amount of nutrients to provide support directly back to the ground. Sometimes directly to the tree from which it came. Other times that leaf is blown far, far away from its home and has only been a consumer of that tree. Not a producer that gives back to which it came.

We're all given one chance. Just one chance to experience life and await for that delicate fall. I couldn't help but begin to allow myself to grieve over future life experiences. Events that naturally occur in life that I would miss and the questions that my absence brought. Knowing my chance, my fall, may indeed be here.

My boys growing up without a father. My Dad was, and still is so important in my life. Who will teach them to become men? Who will model for them how to love and respect their wife? Who will teach them the values of our family? The values of our faith? Will they find and have the wisdom to stay on the right path? If not, can heaven really be so wonderful if I can't spend it with them? All of them?

Who's going to walk Natalie down the aisle? Will someone new be sitting next to Claire? Why, on what's supposed to be the happiest day of her life, should Natalie have to sort through those confused emotions because she thinks I'm not with her? Have I loved and taught her enough to know I will always be with her? Will she even remember me? What do I remember from being 4 years old? Not a lot. Damn. Not a lot.

The practical, mental debate I had the hardest time shaking was, should this not end well, where I would be buried. The cemetery next to the park made sense. It's so close and a convenient way to keep my memory alive. I would hope anyway.

And so the internal debate went something like this:

"How convenient would it be for them to come over after a game and tell me how they did? Or after playing on the playground or the tennis courts like we've done so many times to just stop over to say hi?"

That would be countered with a:

"Are you crazy?! You might as well start making payments to some therapist to help them deal with that. What kid wants to break from the ritual team huddle after a ballgame, grab their little snack, and run over to the cemetery to tell their dead father's grave how they did?"

What a crappy debate to wade through. Dang cancer. That spot of ground right over there may be my permanent resting place on this earth. The very cemetery that I can see from the trail. I'm close enough I can read the names and the dates on the stones. There's so many of them. Hundreds, thousands of them. I often wonder as I pass by the names and dates about their lives. I come back to one question: what did they worry about? And in the end did it really matter? The energy and resources they gave to trivial things in their life. Did all that matter?

The energy and resources we give to trivial things in our lives: does it matter? How different would our lives be, our community be, if all that energy was redirected into something productive. And in every town, big or small, in this country and all over the world for all time there's a simple truth: wherever you find people living you will find people dying.

As one of our cancer doctors said to us "You're mortality rate is 100%. So is mine. So is everyone's. We will all die someday."

For a normal person in a normal life that statement may be a bit unsettling. But as a guy going through cancer it landed softly. Yes, that's right isn't it? We are all someday going to leave this world. And maybe 10 or 100 or 1,000 years from now someone will walk by my stone and glance over my name and dates and wonder about my life. Wonder what I worried about. Wonder if all that worry provided an ounce of benefit to my life.

It's natural to worry. It's part of our DNA. As evident in Proverbs, anxiety has been a problem for people for thousands and thousands of years. It's part of our human weakness.

It's ok to worry and be anxious. It's perfectly natural. But here's the key—you can't stay there. Sort it out. Sift through it. Recognize the parts you can control. Use all the skill and talent and resources you have to take care of that part of the equation. God equipped you with those skills for a reason. That's on us. That's our part.

The rest, the part that's not in our control, we hand over to God. Let Him take care of it. It's what He wants. It's what we need. Then enjoy the peace and grace of knowing you are doing everything you can. You'll adjust as you need to—God gave us critical thinking skills for a reason. But move on. Start today. Don't wait for your leaf to be settling on the ground to know how to live.

*"And can I sail through the changing ocean tides?
Can I handle the seasons of my life?"*

Round 4

**Through many dangers, toils and snares,
I have already come.....**

First song out of chemo
By Dan Klein — March 19, 2014

Amazing Grace.

Great song. Better story.

It was written by John Newton around 1780. John Newton was a minister in the second part of his life. The first part: a sailor on a slave ship delivering slaves across the Atlantic. Next time you hear it listen a bit closer to the words knowing that.

Wherever you've been whatever you've done God is waiting for you. Anxiously waiting.

"Tis Grace that brought me safe thus far, and Grace will lead me home."

Take me home Claire. It's going to be a good round.

Sunday Evening Post
By Dan Klein — March 23, 2014

I'm not sure why but I just assumed the chemo rounds would follow certain predictable patterns. And while there are some similarities I've been surprised at the variance from round to round. Unlike previous rounds where the steroids propped me up for the 24-48 hours after heading out of Vandy this time around I never really got that boost. I just got nauseous—which is not cool.

Early and often. The Rumble dug into his bag of tricks and threw that one at me with everything he had Friday evening. Friday night was by far the worst and got me worried I was in for a very, very long weekend.

The doctors said we shouldn't expect throwing up and to this point they have been right. But, oh, how I longed to be able to do just that for a little reprieve Friday night. But instead I was stuck at the point where you knew— wished— you could go ahead and get it over with.

I tried crackers, Tostito chips, my go-to after chemo Krissy T's soup. Something. Anything. But the same thing would happen about ten minutes later—that watering feeling in your mouth, stomach letting you know it doesn't appreciate your efforts, and heartburn—oh that dang heartburn. And the body rather than rejecting it just wallowed in it. Throw in the metallic taste in your mouth and it's just not the way you want to spend a Friday night.

I was also coming off a pretty rotten second half of strong week. My weight usually fluctuates six and eight pounds from heaviest (usually Tuesday night before chemo) to lightest (Sunday morning after chemo). But this time around I went into chemo at my lightest weight yet. Not good and I knew it. Because I could feel myself just being a little weaker.

By later Friday night I finally convinced myself I was going to force down a boost. Bad idea—body did not like that. Bad idea. Watering mouth combined with that crappy metallic post-chemo taste and stomach screaming is just plain bad. Bad.

As long as I didn't eat or drink I was ok but that's not a long term solution. So I tried to eat and drink what I

could. I remember something from a book about John Mc-
Cain and his time as a POW in Vietnam. When asked how
he survived 5+ years he said he took things ones day at a
time. And when that was too hard he took it one hour at
a time. And when that was too hard it was 30 minutes at
a time and when that was too hard he allowed himself to
breakdown but eventually got back up.

I've called on that in other times in my life—seemingly
important at the time but I couldn't tell you now what was
so important. That's part of the gift of cancer is the awareness of what is important and what is not.

And so I called on that Friday night. I got down to five
minute segments pretty quick. Please God get me through
the next five minutes. Never minute to minute and never
to breakdown status. Five minute segments was as bad as
it got. I was thankful for that. And I was thankful for John
McCain sharing that nugget from his miserable experience
that helped a guy he would never meet and never know
get through a tough night.

And I really wasn't sure how I was going to make it through
the night let alone to Sunday or Monday but that's why I
just focused on the next five minutes. Then the next five
minutes. Then the next.

And, like all other things chemo, it too passed. Thank you
Lord, it passed. And Saturday morning did indeed roll
around and the sun rose on a new day. And I felt a lot
better. I felt well enough to make it to the ballpark later
that morning.

Saturday afternoon rolled around and I darn near felt
good. Good enough to make it to Kereiakes and do a lap
that afternoon and by Sunday evening I was on my way

to Park City to Rock Castle Resort with Matthew to join my good friend Nick and some other guys for mass with Father Steve and a wildgame cookout.

Pretty cool to celebrate mass with eleven good guys, hang out around the campfire, and enjoy a wild game cook-out—especially 24 hours after you were just trying to get through the next five minutes.

Sometimes life is like that. You just have to have enough faith to battle through and turn the corner and see the sunrise on a new day.

Sorry, Father Steve, I didn't try your squirrel stew—medical dietary exemption card played here with authority—even though you shot it (them??) with a bow and arrow. Just not feeling that one Padre.

I feel pretty good. Fatigue is a bit of an issue but that's ok. I can deal with that. Sleep is much improved thanks to a stronger chemical friend and learning how and when my body responds to it. That will take sometime to unwind when this is all said and done but that's months away and I'll deal with that when the time comes.

I'm really feeling pretty good symptom-wise—other than the whole life at five minute interval thing but that was temporary.

Big Week
By Dan Klein — March 31, 2014

Sorry for the radio silence. I hit a bit of a bump in the road last week as fight week wrapped up and strong week started—supposedly started. Let's just say a double digit weight drop over the span of four days is not good for anyone let alone someone going through chemo. And, as most of you already know, I don't have a pound to give— let alone double digit poundage.

That was frustrating and set me back after coming through, or thought I was through, a tough weekend. It's gone and I felt like a million bucks today. I can still function fine most days but as far as feeling fairly close to normal on a good day I got somewhere between three to five hours. Outside of that window I feel ok but at some point I usually just need to shut down physically for an hour or two.

I forced myself not to physically go into work today. I love what I do and the people I work with and my clients. I have a job that I love to get out of bed in the morning to go to and it frustrates me to be limited in my capacity to work. I told Jodi last week I would love to be able to get a forty hour work week in and then laughed and said she would probably love to get *only* a 40 hour week in also. Thanks again Jodi.

So bad news from this cycle:

Some really tough days with Friday right after chemo being when I dropped in what I call the "chemo hole". The Monday-Thursday that followed wasn't a whole lot better but hovered around the five on my scale rather than the 7-pushing-8 Friday night –5 being I'm not capable of functioning normally and 10 being Claire get me to the ER—ASAP.

Significant weight loss but I got my appetite back Friday and have erased a good portion of the deficit. Boy was it good to eat again. My immune system is down so I pick up every little thing like this darn skin-rash-itchy-thing that has popped up on my neck, stomach, back of my hands, and now the tip of my nose. That's high on my list of least favorite things of this experience.

And I officially asked D1 to shelf my membership through September because I know—and have come to terms with the fact—that I simply cannot physically do boot camp. So that's the bad news.

But the good news from this cycle: I feel really good today. So good that I spent the bulk of my day at WKU's graduate library. That's one of my favorite places to really get work done because you basically have a floor to yourself especially on a nice spring day. I made the conscious decision to park close to downtown so I could walk, with my full backpack, up the hill. I know it's not a mile but it has to be close and it felt good to get my heart rate up and breathing hard.

On Saturday my cousin Julie and her family made a quick stop and we had lunch with them at IHOP on their marathon road trip from Florida back to Chicago. Great to see you Julie & Tom. Anytime just let us know and you are welcome in our home for the night or we'll meet you for a quick pit stop. Hope to see you in July at Higgins Lake.

The highlight was my grade school buddies came in for the weekend. My college buddies came back in February. So this weekend my four good friends from growing up in Michigan, three of which I have known since Kindergarten, came to support their old friend. Two of them—Mike and Sean—drove down from Michigan. Larry flew in from Boston and Paul flew in from NYC. We visited the sinkhole at the Corvette Museum, spent a lot of time at the house with the family playing ping pong and basketball which my boys especially loved (thanks guys).

Sunday afternoon Larry, Paul, and I made it up to Mammoth Cave and did Cedar Sink Trail and hit Porky Pig Diner. Poor Paul—in support of Claire, a U of L fan of course, he bought a red Cards shirt and wore it under his unbuttoned shirt (blouse?) and didn't get five steps inside Porky Pig Diner before the nice, older, church going crowd started lobbing their insults at him.

Even the cook told us the price of the buffet just went up. Welcome to MarchMadness in the state of Kentucky.

Larry & Paul flew out Monday morning, so it worked out that the boys and I had tickets to the Predators game Sunday night. We headed home to BG after the game and they headed out to Broadway to experience Nashville and had a hotel room for the night. I'm not sure if they actually slept before their 6:30 a.m. flight.

There was a 6th of our crew, still is and always will be in some ways. Christian died of testicular cancer right after college. Our son Ben—Benjamin Christian—is named in honor of him: Christian Benjamin. I remember making the drive to Michigan to see Christian knowing it would be the last time I saw him on basically a goodbye trip. I believe he found out in February and died in August.

I'm grateful my prognosis is much better and is not as aggressive. I'm grateful this was not a goodbye trip. I'm grateful for my old friends. Thanks again guys.

This Wednesday is our big check in date. THe PET scan was cleared with insurance which means we get a pretty good idea Wednesday how things are going. Extra thoughts and prayers are appreciated. I've done my part, the doctors have done their part, you have done yours in supporting us—thank you again—all I can do is to turn it over to God and then deal with the results. We'll know Wednesday.

My sister Caroline is driving back down from Chicago tomorrow. She insisted Claire and I spend the night in Nashville and have a date night. Thanks Sis. You still look out for your baby brother.

So we're off to Nashville tomorrow evening to get a better idea of what our future holds Wednesday, probably around lunch time. No closing down of bars on Broadway as I have a feeling Larry & Paul did. Just a quiet night together. Not sure what the protocol is for dinner conversation on date night, hours before your PET scan that will pretty much tell you where you stand. I have Claire with me and that's all that matters.

Reflections From the End of the Dock:
Date Night

The calendar has finally turned to April on a beautiful spring day. The house is buzzing with the kids playing with their cousins. Thankfully unaware of the significance of the next 24 hours. We say goodbye to Caroline, still first born and protector, and head out for Nashville. A trip we have come to know all too well.

The protocol for Hodgkin's treatment calls for a pet scan after the 4th round of chemo. That way you can see if the chemo is working. If it is, that's a good sign. A very good sign and you continue on as planned. If not, if the cancer is still there or hasn't shrunk by a certain amount, then you adjust your chemical regiment. You dial it up.

Good Lord there's another level to this?

Oh yes. And it's called salvage chemo. Salvage chemo? I know what regular chemo is. The thought that there is something even called salvage chemo is beyond intimidating.

But we're not worried about that. We're not thinking about that. We're just going to enjoy tonight. Fate doesn't tip its hand. You just have to wait. Then you play whatever cards you're dealt the best you can. We've grown accustomed to this style of play. So tonight it's just us.

We stay at a nice Marriot by the airport. An easy 10 minute drive to Vanderbilt the next morning. There's a nice restaurant in the lobby and we opt for that rather than heading out on the town somewhere. Simple is good. What and where are not as important as who.

No awkward silence. No grand strategy planning of the what-ifs. I just appreciated being with Claire. Just dinner with the most impressive person I have ever met.

"T'was grace that brought us safe thus far.
And grace will lead us home."

Round 5

Don't lose your grip on the dreams of the past...

Off to a Good Start
By Dan Klein — April 2, 2014

We have arrived and are settling in for a long day. PETs at 10, doc at 1:30, chemo at 2:30. If all goes well we're out around 6:00. But chemo is like flying in some ways. The later in the day you are scheduled the more likely you will be delayed. They close at 8:00 and hopefully we'll be done by then.

At Vandy's Cancer Center they have valet parking. Which is really nice but if falls in the medical privilege category. You don't want medical privileges. You dont want to get moved to the front of the line. You dont want special arrangements to make sure you get to the doctor or the lab or radiology ASAP. You dont want to be on a first name basis with everyone from the receptionist to your doctors.

It's nice and very convenient but you don't want it. And you don't want valet parking.

It's all a subtle way of saying what you have is bad enough to warrant special privileges. Better to wait or park three blocks away or not get scheduled for two weeks which doesn't fit real well with your schedule but, believe me, take that as a good sign rather than an inconvenience.

And for those of you who have seen me lately, or on a regular basis can probably tell my hair is much thinner but I still look pretty healthy. Darn near normal I may even say.

So, as the good Lord always does with perfect timing, He was there to greet us this morning when I got out of the driver's side door and the valet parking attendant honestly asked "Are you a patient?" Off to a good start!

Reflections from the Cancer Center Chapel: The Stone

Head phones in, I drift in and out of sleep. I am gently tugged back into consciousness every forty-five seconds or so as the PET scan shifts with that mechanical hum. I lay on the narrow long table as the scan gradually covers the area of focus. I'm at peace. Whatever happens will happen. There's nothing I can do about it. Just wait.

After about thirty minutes the scan is complete. The two radiation therapist help me off the table and escort me back to the make shift waiting area where Claire is sitting alone. We exchange a look, a soft hug, and an exhale as we await the next several hours for the PET to be read and the results shared with us.

We have some time before our appointment with David and Leslie for the big reveal to see what the future holds. Is there a future? Is the chemo working? Is it business as usual chemo today? Or is today fight for your life salvage chemo? Please Lord, not salvage chemo.

There is a place at Vanderbilt, as I'm sure there is at most cancer centers, I keep in the back of my mind as a resource for times when I'm struggling with something. The chapel. Inside that chapel is the altar, a stone table.

We are alone in this small and quiet space. A small number of short pews illuminated by dim, appropriate lighting. Candles in rows on either side burning at different levels marking time for their owner's visit.

We approach the stone altar and kneel. I close my eyes. I become aware, can almost hear and certainly feel, the prayers that have been laid down on this stone. Oh, the magnitude of what has been laid on this stone. Most stone is left in its natural place and undisturbed by human hands. Other stone get set in the sides of buildings or homes. But this stone, oh the weight this stone has to bear.

This stone, on any given day, will have the gamut of emotions laid down on top of it. The pleading. The thanking. The questioning. The surrendering. The anger.

Where do I place my prayer among all of that? Thankfully it's not up to me to decide where it ranks with all the others. The prayers of spouses, like us. The prayers of adult children for their aging parents. The prayers of parents for their young children, laid down on this stone.

I humbly place my prayer on that stone of deep emotion. Aware of what the next few hours hold. This is it. Really? Is this it? Are all of my dreams of the past just that? Did all of it really happen this fast? Or do I, can I please Lord, get another chance to get back on my feet?

PET is negative!!!
By Claire Klein — April 2, 2014

A long day at Vandy is much more tolerable when you have good news! Thanks to Caroline, one of Dan 's sisters, we started this trip with a peaceful evening staying in a hotel here in Nashville. She is at home manning seven kids. Thank you, Caroline!

Dan had a PET scan this morning with time to kill afterwards before meeting with the doctor. We found comfort by visiting the chapel before heading outside. What a beautiful day to walk on campus and have a nice lunch. We met with the doctor at 1:15. Praise The Lord, there is NOTHING glowing in DAN's chest!! No signs of cancer.

This was the news that we were waiting to hear. Unfortunately, this does not change the course of treatment (even though we jokingly ask every time), so we must continue four more months of chemo and radiation. Studies and research prove that this is the course. They expect this PET to be negative and if not the prognosis is not as good.

The good news is that it is negative, and 92% chance to make it to 5 years...in which it should NEVER come back.

We have finally been taken back to the infusion room, and Dan is preparing for his fight with the Red Devil (one of the red meds). He continues to be a real trooper. Thank you for your continued outpouring of love, support, and prayers!! We are so appreciative!! And thank you for the extra love showered on our kiddos!! XO, Claire

Note from Claire

When I was pregnant with our first child, I remember telling Dan that I would never forget what life was like before having children. We had so many friends who had kids, and we always heard them say that they couldn't remember what life was like before kids. I loved kids and couldn't wait to have my own, but I was always going to remember life before them. Dan and I spent a lot of time together. We often went to the park to play tennis, played coed softball and flag football, had parties with our work friends, and the best was staying up later on the weekends and forcing ourselves out of bed by 8:30 or 9 so that we didn't waste our day. Dan still mentions all those Sundays that he laid on the couch watching football with his head in my lap. I would scratch his head and read a book. We had no interruptions. We all know that the logisitics of these events change when kids arrive.

We, of course, adapted and were able to continue with some of our activities, but I still have a good recollection of life before children. And as our family has grown, and we wouldn't change that for the world, we have realized that taking time for ourselves, though infrequent, is really important. I find myself at times throwing so much energy into the kids that Dan is neglected more than he should be. He usually has one or two business conferences a year that we try to attend. It is these three night get aways, that help us to leave the stresses of four kids with Gamm and Pop and a relief sitter to refocus on each other. When we were able to head to Nashville the night before the PET scan, knowing that our four were in the loving hands of Aunt Caroline, we forgot about cancer and all the other activities for a brief time. We were able to sit and enjoy a nice meal together. We were able to bring it back to where it all started...the two of us.

First Song out of Chemo
By Dan Klein — April 2, 2014

"Eye of the Tiger" by Survivor.

What else??

Crossing the state line back into good old Kentucky. My driver is cute. And smiling. And so am I :)

Slept like a rock last night. I had peace with however the cards fell today. But very thankful for a clean report. Thankful is an understatement.

I've learned that we are really good about going to God with our problems but we don't always share our joys and answered prayers. That's not a cool relationship. Who wants only someone's toxicity?

So before the first call, post, text went out I went to Him to allow him to feel the joy and pressure release.

Ahh, exhale. Thank you Dear Lord.

Just need to let them pummel my body for the next four months. Bring it, Rumble. "Is that all you got?" said Ali to Foreman.

"Went the distance now I'm not going to stop just a man and his will to survive"

Strong Week
By Dan Klein — April 10, 2014

When I start getting texts asking me if I'm ok I realize I've not updated the site so here we go.

I am feeling awesome. Putting in full days for the most part. Side effects this round are minimal or I'm just getting used to them—if such a thing is possible. Hair is still hanging in—sort of. Thin and a bit spotty but still there. Sorry Dad and brothers, I may not join your bald club after all.

I will share that after getting the good news about the PET scan I have found/allowed myself to start going back to living outside the moment. And boy is living in the moment this really neat place. It's just a peaceful place and it's the secret to life. Be where your feet are. Part of the gift of cancer.

We got the results on Wednesday and by the weekend I was starting to think ahead, which is not completely a bad thing. That's part of being a responsible adult. Certain things you plan for. But I was starting to worry. Worry about the things we worry about. Or at least I do. And I recognized that and became aware of it and I didn't like it. But what I really didn't like was that I was starting to essentially take back the load from God that I had dumped on him.

"Thanks for your help when I needed you. I've got it from here" kind of thing.

That's not cool and that's not the basis for any healthy relationship. You take the crap. I'll take the good stuff.

Please be on standby if I need you again. I'm not comfortable with being on either side of that relationship. As someone much smarter than me has said to me in any relationship if one party is unhappy it's just a matter of time before all parties are unhappy.

But it felt so good to feel capable again and be back to somewhat normal mode. So I talked to Him about it. I let Him know I was struggling with that. That I wanted to move closer and that's where I want to stay. I spent a little more time in Proverbs. I spent a little more time in the gospels. But I was still struggling. How quickly I reverted to my old ways when I got the clean report that there was no cancer left in my body. More going through the motions than being all in. It's that workout you know you have to do but you're just putting in the time and not really leaning into it to get anything out of it. It's the salad you buy for lunch, with the large coke, for your diet.

That's not who I am when I'm at my best. And I know faith is not a gene. It's a muscle. Just like attitude. You have to constantly work on it, otherwise you fall out of shape and atrophy. So I'm pushing to get closer. And I'm worrying. And come Monday morning I'm still there. Pushing. Worrying. Leaning in, but I have a pretty good headwind of life—I got things to do at work, I got a pile of medical bills that I have to go through, I've got to get three kids to practices on other ends of town, I need to help Claire out more, the garage is a wreck and it's no wonder why John can't find his glove because I've allowed the garage to become a wreck but I'm getting frustrated at him.

I've got this, I've got that. I'm allowing my mind to run the endless loop of these first world problems that I am devoting resources to that deserve some shelf space and attention but not to the extent that I'm allocating them.

And dog gone it, if Monday morning the guy in front of me at McDonalds is taking forever. I'm a fan of efficiency and when the sign in the drive thru says please have correct change ready, dang it all, get your change ready while you wait. He's taking so long that the two cars in front of him are gone. Out of the parking lot. He's at the pay window. I'm behind him. And nobody is in front of him and I'm running behind—which of course is his fault. I rarely get frustrated when driving. Not never, but rarely. But I'm frustrated.

Finally, the guy pulls ahead and I pull up to the window. No, I roll to the window because my correct change is ready and I like to see if I can never come to a complete stop. Just roll by slowly, hand over the money—correct change because the sign told me—and never actually stop just roll on up to the next window.

Yup. There my sign was waiting for me. Thank you Lord for the not-so-subtle sign. Thanks to whoever that guy was who for whatever reason felt in his heart that morning to buy the guy behind him breakfast. He didnt know I was struggling. But he felt in his heart to buy breakfast for the person behind him.

I don't expect Jesus or Moses or St. Peter to descend into the drive thru at McDonalds in front of my car and walk up to that smiling lady and hand over money (correct change of course) with their big staff and white robe flapping in the wind, nod at me as they ascend upward, for my sign that He understands and He's with me.

I've come to understand that God works through us—me and you—to reveal Himself. And it's everyday. We just have to look for it. Or, better yet, we have to listen for how He wants to work through us for someone else.

I don't know what kind of day the person behind me was having on Tuesday morning. But I made sure I bought their breakfast. And I promise you I got more out of that than the $3.78 it cost me.

It's strong week. When you walk closely with the Lord every week is strong week.

Reflections From the End of the Dock: Life Push-Ups

There are certain things that if I do them on a regular basis everything else seems to fall into place: Begin and end each day in prayer. Log time every day in the classroom of silence. Mentally be where my feet are. Exercise on a regular basis. Be proactive towards the future but live today with an awareness of outward focus.

When I do all those things I am at my best. I'm sharp mentally, physically, emotionally, and spiritually. I do in fact walk closer with the Lord and life just clicks.

But for whatever reason it is easy to slip out of those habits. And when one of those pieces begins to wiggle loose the others are usually not far behind. Even though I know those things allow me to be at my best there are stretches where I allow the routine to break down. The longer that routine stays out of order the harder it can be to get back online. Falling out of order is not always a conscious decision. Rather a combination of events.

I think life can be like that. If you stop and look around and take inventory of your life maybe it's exactly what you had planned. Or maybe it's just the linear progression of a lifetime of smaller individual decisions that landed you where you are. As I have heard it said, ask yourself where you want to be in one year from now. Paint yourself a picture of what the ideal life looks like for you. What do you want your life to look like in 12 months from this day? And if you don't end up at that place, whose fault is it? These are the things you think about when you wait for the results of your PET scan. Await to hear the words salvage chemo.

The mental, physical, emotional, and spiritual parts of our lives need consistent exercise. They are not a gene. You have to work them. They have to get in shape and be kept in shape. Constantly. Neglect them, allow one part to atrophy, and you're inviting trouble in. It's a lot like good hygiene. You take a shower every day to rinse off whatever has accumulated. Skip one day no big deal. Start stringing together days or a couple of weeks and the filth builds. Often times noticed by others before we become aware of it ourselves.

I recognize that in order to move closer to that ideal life it begins with the motivation to consistently do the little things right. Not monumental shifts. Working and pushing every day. Just the daily choices that accumulate over time. Those daily life push-ups keep you in shape. They form your habits. Your habits form your character and ultimately your life. And when the storms of life begin to blow your life muscles are ready. *"You must fight just to keep them alive."*

Round 6

There's always going to be
another mountain.
I'm always going to want
to make it move.
Always going to be
an uphill battle.
Sometimes I'm going to
have to lose...

First Song out of Chemo
By Dan Klein — April 16, 2014

"It's the Climb" by Hannah Montana

I know, I know. I must say I'm not a Miley Cyrus fan these days. I suppose it's a lot to ask a young person in her position to make good sound responsible decisions. Especially when you live under a microscope.

It makes me appreciate my parents allowing me to make my own mistakes and grow from them in my own time and space. Or maybe when your child number five in five years it just happens.

But it's a good jingle and the lyrics fit:

"There's always going to be another mountain. I'm always gonna to want to make it move. Always going to be an uphill battle. Sometimes I'm going to have to lose.... The struggles I'm facing. The chances I'm taking. Sometimes may knock me down. But no, I'm not breaking."

Boy is that chemo. Chemo's no joke and I greatly dislike it. I physically feel bad just thinking of it or catching a smell of the soap Vandy uses. I recognize its a means to the end but it still is a horrible process to work through.

It's the climb—or the grind as I call it. Just the day to day, sometimes five minutes to five minutes, battle in the trenches. Sometimes it's easy. Sometimes it's downright unbearable to the point where I text my accountability buddies and ask them to pray.

I know that is the weekend that lays ahead of me. I hope

it's on the easy side. Its Easter weekend after all. I know this is where I have to grind it out and deal with it. Get over this mountain. Get to the next mountain. I know The Rumble will come out swinging. I know I can bend but not break and come Monday be able to stand.

The grind is coming whether I want it or not. Might as well embrace the challenge and take away from it whatever I can.

As a quote on my board says in the MCRR "I'm growing through cancer not going through cancer."

Bracing for impact.....

Almost home. And my driver is awfully cute:)

Round 6 Recap
By Dan Klein — April 22, 2014

Not a fan of Round six. This was a rough one. I'm going to tip my hat to The Rumble this round and try again next time. You would think there would be some consistencies through the treatments so you could have an idea of what to expect. I chalk that up to being one of cancer's dirty little tricks. It's such an unfair opponent and it knows nor appreciates any type of civilized rules of engagement.

Moving forward—slower than I'd like this round but moving forward. Halfway through chemo and that's good. Another twelve weeks of this seems like a lot and frankly is more than I want to think about. But I'm appreciative that there is indeed a finish line. I'm aware some people dont have a finish line that close or there is no finish line in their battle and that would be hard for me to process.

It will pass and will be here quickly and I know that. I'm trying not to think ahead to six more rounds of this stuff. Just today.

The first thing the doctor usually wants to know is if there is any numbness or tingling in my hands or fingers. To this point that's been a no. But I've got that going on this round and it's really irritating.

My faithful chemo buddies—nausea and fatigue—are hanging around longer and that's making things uncomfortable. I'm trying to eat but it's just not that easy. I promised the doctor I would come back next Wednesday and with some weight back on. Going into strong week I'm in pretty good position to accomplish that especially if I can get nausea to go home for a few days.

If given a choice between the two I'll gladly take fatigue. While we're sending people home I'd also love to get rid of the horrible chemo taste. Oh how I dislike the chemo taste.

The good things about round 6 is I'm a week out of chemo and one round closer. I'm thankful for that. I'm just going to enjoy my strong week and I'll do my best to not start thinking about Round 7 until next Wednesday morning on the way to Nashville.

Gearing Up for Round 7
By Dan Klein — April 29, 2014

Halfway home through chemo. Thank you, Lord. Thank you, Claire. And thanks to everyone else for carrying me this far. The prayers, the notes, the meals, the visits, the posts, the emails and texts, the everythings. Thank you.

THE BRIDGE

I will forever be thankful to you.

I'd like to have some grand motivational halftime locker room speach to get me pumped up for the next six rounds but I still am at my best in day-to-day mode. At first, the thought of being halfway was great—and then I started thinking that means I got to do it all over again. Dang it!

Six—such an easy word to say and write and type. But to get my hands around six more trips to Vandy. Six more rounds of chemo. Six more trips on the unpredictable roll-ercoaster ride that is cancer. Too much. Knowing the next six probably won't be any easier than the first six is too much to think about.

So I don't. I'm just thinking about round seven. I need to take care of what I can control to get me through round seven. After a really bad fight week I felt great today and pretty darn good the last 5-6 days. Sleeping pretty well. I did three brisk laps at Kereiakes this morning. I'm going to guess I will weigh in 10lbs heavier tomorrow than I did two weeks ago.

After such a lousy fight week, I figured I better do some-thing about it and have been pounding down food and boost and have walked every day for the last five days, rain or shine. Got in almost a full day at work today—boy do I love to be at work.

After dinner tonight, we played wiffle ball in the backyard in the rain. I'm still faster than my boys but they are gain-ing on me. And they still can't hit my knuckle ball.

Normalcy is a good thing around here and trades at a high premium. I think the fact that my hair is somewhat hang-ing on has helped with that. John told us at the beginning when my hair fell out he would get a buzz cut. Last week, without telling me anything about it, he got his buzz cut. That's my guy. Some days you'd like to put your kids on the curb for the city to come pick up and other days you just want to freeze time and stay with them like they are forever.

I know it's the science of chemotherapy—poison the body to the point it can take it, then allow it to rebuild just long enough to be able to take another dose. Man would I love to have one more day to feel this good. The watery taste in the mouth is almost gone. The horrible metal taste is almost gone. The stomach isn't "right" but it's manageable. The horrible headache is gone. That way-too-full-after-Thanksgiving-meal feeling is mostly gone. The fingers still tingle but stopped waking me up in the middle of the night.

You just get back to your feet and it's time. Oh, for one more day to feel this good. I'll have those days I know when this is all over. They're coming and I hope I remember this lesson. I cant see how I could possibly forget it.

That's part of that gift of cancer. Halfway through chemo (not thinking about radiation—we'll deal with that later) and I am already aware that at the end I'm coming out of this with more in my pocket than the cost. To want what you have and to have the awareness of what's important —there's no price tag for that. One hundred and eighty days of feeling bad for a lifetime of perspective.

To me I call that a deal.

Just tomorrow. Just round 7. We'll get through that and then start working up to the next round.

Reflections From the End of the Dock: The Grind Line

I enjoy long term planning and the excitement that comes from visualizing the what-ifs. Figuring out where you are right now and where you want to be. The A and the Z of planning. But it's the B to the Y that's tough. The execution, the energy, and the endurance to make it. That's the hard part. That's the grind.

Growing up in Michigan I was, of course, a Detroit Red Wings fan. They currently hold the record in all professional sports for the longest consecutive post season appearances. For the last 25 years they have made the playoffs. In a 15 year stretch of that time they won 4 Stanley Cups and lost in the finals 3 times. But prior to that period the Red Wings were better known as "The Dead Things". Making the playoffs only twice in one 20 year stretch of that dark time.

How do you turn around a culture of losing into one of the most respected franchises in all of professional sports? How do you turn failure into a dynasty? There's never just one factor and it won't happen overnight. Sure there were great players and strategic moves. There were some lucky breaks along the way. But the concept that epitomizes it all was the Grind Line.

In hockey you have certain groups of players that typically play at the same time called a line. Usually your 1st line is your best scoring line followed by the 2nd and 3rd line. In the mid-90's, in the early stages of the turnaround, the Detroit Red Wings had a 4th line that came to be known as "The Grind Line."

These were guys with probably more heart than talent. Less teeth than even your average hockey player. They didn't fill up the stat sheet. They weren't the high draft picks or the guys who got all the headlines. They were guys who just put on their hard hats and went to work. Every day. They not only knew their role they embraced it. They went into the corners to dig out loose pucks. They laid down their body to block shots. They stood in front of the opposing team's goalie and took the beatings with pride that come with finding yourself in that highly protected piece of ice.

In short, they did whatever it took to get it done. Last minute of the finals or random second period of the first month of the season. They set the tone. For the better part of a decade they did the little things night in and night out. Not only does that prove to be effective for them but it begins to rub off on others.

You can have the hall of fame talent with names like Yzerman and Lidstrom. You can have the innovative strategy and concepts like the Left Wing Lock. But if you don't do the little things all of that is for not. You must recognize the things that you know you need to do but just don't want to. As Steven Covey so clearly lays out: "Effective people don't want to do certain things any more than non-effective people. They just dislike the effects of not doing those things more so than doing them."

Those little things that are easy to overlook. Those little things that need to be done on a consistent basis to put yourself in a position to be consistently successful. Those little things that cause other people to drop out of the race. You not only have to recognize those things but prioritize and even embrace them. As your own head coach standing behind the bench of life in a hard fought game when you know things are difficult there's only one thing to say:

"Grind Line, take over."

"The struggles I'm facing. The chances I'm taking.
Sometimes may knock me down.
But no, I'm not breaking."

Round 7

**Sometimes in life we all have pain.
We all have sorrows....**

First Song out of Chemo
By Dan Klein — April 20, 2014

"Lean on Me" by Bill Withers.

Somethings don't need an explanation.

We got down to Vandy early and will be home by the time the kids get home. That's nice. I packed on the weight as I promised the doc. Hit my 10lb goal and then some. Actually weighed in heavier than my weigh in before round one. Double digit weight swings do funny things to a body and I got to even out the swings as best I can.

They added an additional steroid to the IV to help this round. The dreaded cumulative effect of chemo I'm afraid is creeping in. We'll make it. Hopefully by next Wednesday strong week is coming in for its welcomed landing.

Ding ding. Round 7 has begun. Going to crawl in the chemo hole. The steroids prop me up for a couple of days and come the weekend we'll let the poison do what it's suppose to do and then move forward.

Round 7 Update
By Dan Klein — May 9, 2014

Strong week is in. But coming in slowly. The first half of round 7 was certainly easier than round 6 and that was very welcome relief because round 6 was a tough one. And I was looking forward to this week being a better strong week as well but I'm still waiting for the uplift. It just doesnt want to come.

Nausea and fatigue continue to be the companions I can't seem to shake. I don't know what the right term is in the sequence when you go from being tired, to fatigued, to exhausted, to whatever that final term is but I'd say I'm knocking on that final term.

I took Natalie to Walmart the other day and I found myself being intimidated by Walmart. That's something when you go "huh, never thought I'd say that." But I can see why people who have a hard time getting around can feel that way. Where do I park and where do I need to go inside the store so I can get in, get what I need, and get back to the car.

Intimidated by Walmart? Go figure.

Cancer's latest dirty trick is a common one to a lot of people—lower back pain. It started a few weeks ago being fairly mild and then the last week or so has entered into wake-up-at-night kind of pain. That's pretty ingenuous on its part because for me the best way to avoid lower back pain is to be active. But on the other hand, the easiest way to manage through fatigue and nausea is to be inactive. It also disrupts sleep which was getting better. Dang cancer.

Right now the back pain is trumping the nausea and fatigue and I'm trying to walk and stretch and ice but it just doesn't want to get better. I got some pretty decent meds and they don't seem to put a dent in it. I got to solve that one and solve it quick because I have about 70 more days (but who's counting??) through chemo and how I've felt the last week or so is not how I plan to spend those days. I'll solve it.

But the clock ticks and days go by. Time waits for no man.

I always thought of that as a bad thing but I think of that often and appreciate that it is working for me now. We are one round closer and that's good.

I knew May and June would be the tough months. The grind is living up to its name. Grinding. Head down. Pushing through. One foot after another. One day at time. Get through this round and get to the next. Check it off the list. Last long enough for it to get tired of picking on me and go away. Endure.

Reflections From the End of the Dock:
Donuts at the Door

There were a couple of things that I would see at the cancer center that bothered me. One of those was the people standing on the sidewalk in their hospital gowns, rolling IV stand next to them, smoking. I don't get that. I don't know the level of that addiction so I try to have some compassion. But that's effort for me. Why on earth would you knowingly increase your chances by any fraction of dealing with this monster?

The other thing that stood out to me, and, believe it or not, much more unsettling than the cancer smokers were the taxi cabs. Maybe for some people it just made better logistical sense to take a cab. Maybe for some people they are just being really considerate and giving their caregiver a day off. My hunch, my fear, is that some of those people had no choice. They went through cancer alone.

I'm sure over time some parts of our journey with cancer will fade from memory. But not that. Not the frail cancer patient getting helped out of the back seat of a cab by the driver to walk into the cancer center. All alone.

Such a stark contrast to what we experienced. It made me incredibly appreciative and aware of the people who allowed us to lean on them. And how important it is to seek out and allow other people to lean on you. How blessed we were to have this incredible support system just construct itself around our family. No real thought or strategy on our part. People just offered to help in whatever way they could. Whatever we needed someone was always there. Our immediate as well as extended family near and far. Old friends and new friends. The kids' coaches helping out with rides and teachers spending a little extra time. And someone gets dropped off in a cab?

People we didn't even know praying for us, offering masses for us, and lighting candles in churches we will never walk into. And someone has to sit in the chemo waiting room alone?

The meal sign up schedule put together that within a couple of weeks had six months filled. The gift cards for a meal or a tank of gas. The packages that would just show up on the front porch. Sometimes with a loving message from a friend or relative. Sometimes with no name or card. Just an anonymous touch of grace. And yet someone has to climb into the back seat of a taxi cab after getting pummeled by chemo and head home to deal with it all alone.

Life is not fair. Why we get so much and others get so little. Or nothing. We have a saying with our friends: "Divide our struggles and multiply our joys." I think when we're so worried about our own challenges we miss out on opportunities to serve others and help them to divide their struggles. It's easy to get so wrapped up in our own little worlds and what we think of as problems or challenges that we can totally miss out on helping others. I realized very early on in my tenure at the cancer center that compared to others I didn't have problems. Yet we received so much love and support.

When you are on the receiving end of that level of grace you realize something. It doesn't have to be a grand act. More so just the small things. A meal or someone picked up for a game. A carton of ice cream or gas card. The act itself was extremely helpful and appreciated. But it was the love and kindness that those acts represent that was the real gift.

That's why seeing a cab hurts. It's symbolic. Evidence of a lonely journey. No one should have to experience cancer, but if you do you certainly shouldn't be alone. Yet people go through all sorts of struggles alone. For whatever reason the private battles of life that either by choice or circumstance people take on by themselves. Nobody to divide those struggles with. Nobody to sit next to them while they hold their little buzzer waiting for their turn. Nobody to lean on when life's poison begins that steady drip.

Just as a constant headwind of life can wear you down a constant tailwind can pick you up and push you through. Through our entire treatment that tailwind was always there. It was best represented by a little white box that magically appeared on our front porch every Saturday morning. Throughout treatment a donut fairy would leave a box of a dozen donuts at our front door. He or she knew everybody's favorite. He or she made sure there were two of each. Just like going to get the paper on Saturday morning the kids knew the white box with their special breakfast would be there.

Claire and I will both tell you one of the biggest blessings that came from cancer was the gift of our kids witnessing so much love and support. And they don't question when we in turn do things for others. When we make the symbolic donuts at the door gesture. For them it is just the way the world works. You and I may know that's not always the case in a world that is sometimes harsh. But it's how their world works. That's a gift from cancer.

"Lean on me when you're not strong
And I'll be your friend, I'll help you carry on."

Round 8

**I'm no stranger to the rain
But there'll always be tomorrow
And I'll beg, steal, or borrow
a little sunshine..**

Round 8 (Has Begun Early)
First song out of chemo
By Dan Klein — May 13, 2014

"I'm No Stranger to the Rain" by Keith Whitley.

Good old Keith Whitley.

We went a day early this round for scheduling reasons. We discovered Tuesdays are the day to get chemo at Vandy. Checked in at 8:10 and walked out by 2:00. Checked in with my friend, Fannie, who always calls me "babe" and said again today after her usual "Ok babe, what's your full name and date of birth?" shook her head and said that she still thinks I'm just a boy.

I like Fannie.

Feeling a bit worse right after chemo as the rounds go on. A hard feeling to describe other than just bad. Wasn't up for the usual post on the ride home. Just needed to get home.

But yes indeed my driver was cute—even though in the car she likes to grab what little leg hair I have left and say "I wonder if this would just come out if I pulled it? Huh, sure enough."

She's also lobbying for the head shaving to occur. Apparently the patchy-tennis-ball-fuzzy-style is not in this season. As my mother would say it's a good thing you're cute dear.

Only four more trips down there for chemo. That's encouraging. That's very encouraging. I did get a bit of an uplift the last 48 hours—thank you for your prayers and warm wishes. And while I'm being thankful, I'm just incredibly grateful and humbled by the acts of kindness that we continue to receive. What a wonderful experience and lesson to us and to our kids in how you can make a positive impact on someone's life when they're going through a struggle.

Very humbling. I don't know how I will ever adequately and appropriately express that. I very much look forward to getting back on the other side of the caregiver relationship and start chipping away and paying that debt of love and goodwill forward.

I have given myself a bit of a gift now that we are getting close. I've allowed myself to look ahead. Just a peak at getting my life back to normal. Boy does that look good! That's been really nice. This was the right time to allow that. I know the next 60 days will be the hardest but knowing it's getting closer and closer is awesome.

Medical update: four more rounds of chemo with the last one scheduled for Monday, July 7th. Oh how I long for that moment when I walk out the doors at Vandy on that day. It can be 110 degrees or a driving rain storm. Doesn't matter. That is a moment that is coming and I will have my quiet moment with Claire knowing that the worst part —physically anyway—is behind us.

Then just give chemo and The Rumble its final 7-10 days and start the permanent uplift. Ahh!!

Three weeks later on July 28 we do another scan and make sure I am still clean as a whistle and use that for the radiologist to determine the radiation field. The next day, Tuesday July 29th, we begin the radiation phase and do that every day for three weeks. If all goes well we finish radiation on Friday, August 15th. Ahh!!

Five to six weeks later we do another PET scan to confirm, hopefully, that I am cancer free. From there, after one kick ass party (sorry Mom), I go back every three months for awhile, then six months for awhile, and then annually for PET scans. Remission is two years with no cancer returning and cure is five years of clean PET scans. Great big Ahh!!!

Five years sounds like a long time but if I'm not dealing with chemo that is no problem. It's just a matter of periodically going through the mental waiting game of hoping and praying and trusting in God and good medicine every time the doctor pokes their head in the room after a scan with hopefully a big smile and a big hug.

Weight is good. Weighed in at the same level as last round which was actually higher than my initial weigh in at Vandy. That was after the first week of discovering the cancer. Not recommending but there's a crash diet—get told you have cancer and your appetite goes away quickly and you shed poundage in a hurry.

I've just made up my mind that regardless of how it feels, food is going in. Take that cancer!

Got in some good walks last week—a couple of five milers and even got in some running. Fatigue and nausea I can find a way to push through but I got to say the whole lower back pain thing can shut me down. That's just not an option. So with the help of my own personal physical therapist, who is really cute even though she pulls my leg hairs, we're solving that one and it's already better.

Walking, stretching, icing, heating, etc.

Fingers are better. Just a little swollen but very little if any tingling. Mouth is a pain. It has been from the get go and it's just part of it. It's not nearly as bad at its worst but it is just a pain in the you know what.

The new major sideeffect development this go around is what I call "X-Box thumb." Man does that hurt! John and I are playing a full NHL 2014 hockey season on the X-Box and I may have to go on the disabled list, which incidentally would only help our team because I'm really bad. Really bad. Way too many control options. Give me the old Nintendo with four buttons and a joystick and I'm good. But there's like twenty different buttons on these things.

We're having fun. Sometimes I find myself checking the time to see when school is out so we can get in a game or two. Homework can wait. I've even been spending some time on the XBox doing practice drills (to no benefit so far) when I'm home alone—take the good with the bad with cancer.

If I can walk five miles through nausea and fatigue I can play XBox. Our goal is to make the playoffs—we're getting better and the NHL season, like chemo, is a long grind. One game at a time. One stinking control feature at a time. We're 2-9 and currently holding down the cellar.

So tonight I just wait. I wait for the call from chemo to come. I wait for the worst part of chemo. It will probably come around Thursday. The three to five days out from getting that toxic blend pumped into my body and how every system in my body gets together and figures out how they want to handle it and who is going to take the major blows this round and who gets the round off.

I've become very comfortable and reliant on a concept that I've always tried to keep at the core of my attitude: I don't always have control over what happens to me but I always, always, have control over how I respond.

That's my corner. That's where I can be in charge. That's where I'm going to dwell. We're getting closer. Even the really bad days move us one day closer. The picture of Ali looking over George Foreman while Foreman lays on the mat is on my wall in the MCRR and I know that moment is coming.

Hunkering down and going to get through Round 8.

Strong Week has Begun
By Dan Klein — May 21, 2014

I am eight days out from Round 8 treatment and feel pretty darn good. Round 8 was a tough one. May be the toughest yet. First few days it was just my usual chemo side-effect friends hanging out with me. Saturday evening The Rumble flexed his muscles and reminded me of who is really in charge.

It was pretty close to a shut down for 48 hours. No fun. For the first time I almost asked Claire to take me to the hospital.

I knew/hoped it was just a matter of time and really did not want to go to the hospital. And then it eventually lifted. I woke up Tuesday morning feeling halfway normal and by Tuesday evening I felt pretty darn good. I received a nice lift Sunday when I opened a package that my old high school friend, Molly Burns, sent me. She reached out to some of our old classmates and made them aware of what was going on. Molly had them send her cards and notes which she put in a package and forwarded to me. It was a welcome reprieve to sit on the deck Sunday and go through those and see the names of old friends and smile as I sorted through old memories.

To my old friends from Catholic Central High School in Grand Rapids, Michigan: thank you so much. Your words of support, encouragement, and prayer were the perfect medicine in the middle of that rough patch that was Round 8. Thank you for your kindness. That was really nice.

I'm not yet ready to start thinking about Round 9. I know there's just four more rounds, but that's too much for me to get my hands around. Four rounds is too much for me to take in one bite.

Not a fan of chemo. I'm just going to enjoy today. I'm going to enjoy being able to walk and not feel like I'm constantly walking upstream. I'm going to enjoy that terrible chemo taste slowly leaving so I can taste something other than that horrid blend of medicine, metal, and cleaning supplies.

I had the best strawberry last night. I just stood at the kitchen sink and had to tell Claire about it. Oh was it good to taste something good. I get to enjoy six more days of this and I'm really look forward to it. I also know that moves me six days closer to the finish line. It's coming.

Reflections From the End of the Dock: Serenity Prayer

L ife can be tough. Don't I know it. How easy is it to start as-
signing blame. Blaming our situation on things outside our
control. Buying into all the reasons why it's ok to complain and
all the reasons to blame our condition on something or somebody else. It's easy to fall prey to this mentality and granting
those outside things to have even more control. Easier than just
accepting those things and digging in our heels and focusing
on what we can control. How easy, yet how difficult, is it to live
the Serenity Prayer.

Lord, grant me the serenity to accept the things
I cannot change,

Courage to change the things I can,
And wisdom to know the difference.

There is no benefit to worrying about something outside our control. Zero benefit to allowing the endless loop of anxiety to replay over and over again in our heads. Whether we are aware of it or not, worrying about those things negatively impact many aspects of our lives. Our mood and certainly our health. Even our relationships are put at risk. It can ruin our nights – which can then ruin our days. It can become a vicious cycle.

Someone once told me our lives are like a piece of music. Complete with an introduction and an ending. Different tempos for different periods. We all have notes that reach high on the scale—our wedding, the birth of a child, a great career move. And we all have those that fall far below—the death of a loved one, a job loss, a cancer diagnosis. Our lives composed as a song. Cancer is not unique to me. Nor is my treatment experience. Millions of people have played that low note. That horrible sound. Yet, while none of our individual notes are unique the aggregate collection and sequence of them make each of our songs unique.

If I could latch on to just one concept it would be the Serenity Prayer. I dont always have a choice over which notes find their way onto my song. But I always have the choice how I play them.

And I'll put this cloud behind me
That's how the man designed me
To ride the wind
And dance in a hurricane.

Round 9

9 Down
By Claire Klein — May 28, 2014

Hi Faithful Followers! Dan has nine rounds down and three to go. Great thanks to Lukas Forbes for carting Dan to Vandy today. With family having other commitments, one sitter in Europe, and the other still in school, I was unable to go today.

It hurt my heart, but four active kiddos needed some supervision. Joe and Betty Kunkel were so kind to scoop Dan up and bring him home. Dan and (Lukas) were up early for 7:10 am labs, so Dan has been snoozing and just trying to rest. He sure is cute!

A continued feeling of gratitude to all those showing their love, prayers, and support. Especially to those who check on Dan and send him cards, texts, and provide words of encouragement. And thank you too Mickey Logsdon who has graciously started coming over from Glasgow once a week to mow our lawn!!!!!!

I am sure that Dan will journal soon!

Claire

Note from Claire

I am usually in control of the day-to-day operations of our family. I know when we need to leave the house early for one of the kids to get an "Accelerated Reader" award. I am on top of what's for lunch and who will need a lunch packed. I am also aware of field trips or other events at school. At home, I am on top of making sure that uniforms and favorite socks are washed and ready to go.

And then there's the food situation. I have to make sure that there are enough snacks in the cabinet to satisfy everyone after school. It may not be gourmet, but I prepare some type of meal every night so that we aren't eating out. And let's not forget the ice cream. It is an obsession. I never buy any less than 6-10 containers of ice cream at the grocery. Some people splurge on cigarettes or soft drinks. We splurge on ice cream. With Dan's help, I stay on top of practices and game schedules. We keep a liquid chalk board with our weekly schedules hanging in the kitchen.

When Dan started his treatments, I began to realize that I couldn't do all these things without others to lean on. I enjoy staying at the kids' practices to watch and just being there in case one of them needs me. Some nights, two kids would have practices at the same time or within 30 minutes of each other. I realized that I couldn't be in two places at once. Dan gave it everything he had to get to all the boys' games, but I tried to manage as many practices as I could. It was hard to accept that this Supermom needed others to make it. I would reluctantly drive away from the field on to the next practice drop. Or I would depend on another team parent to take one of the boys, and have no association with the event that night. That was hard for me. I have total appreciation for single parenting. It is definitely not a place that I find comfort. I am a much better mother with a partner. Someone to lean on in these wonderful chaotic times. Surrendering to our friends and family was not always easy, but I had to accept that I couldn't do it all.

Nice to see June :)

By Dan Klein — June 2, 2014

Oh, is it nice to turn a calendar to a new month these days! Hard to believe it's June and darn happy to know July is around the corner. Knock on wood this round has slipped by in fairly good order.

Mostly just the usual with no surprises. Thank you Lord—I needed that.

I'm looking forward to the next eight days before round #10. Not even thinking about round #10 yet. Hate to even type it. Just going to enjoy the uplift.

Back in April I decided to sign up for a conference for work knowing it was a bit of a risk. But also knowing having something tangible to look forward to at this stage of the game was sound strategy. So Claire, Matthew, Ben, and & I are heading to Vegas Wednesday am for a quick trip! I'm going to guess I'm not going to venture to far and that's fine with me. Docs don't seem too concerned with my immune system. I think living with four kids has a lot to do with that.

So we're moving forward in good order knowing the finish line is coming closer. I'm not ready to hit the button for the final sprint but at this point I think I still have a little gas in the tank to spend. I expect to need that and expect the last three rounds to be the most difficult. If I catch a break like I did this round than that's a bonus. I'm not betting on cancer letting me off the hook easy. I'm going in with the mindset that the next forty days will be the hardest. And knowing cancer, I know it will be. Dang it all.

I look frequently at my vision board magnet and am starting to visualize the first stop—the end of the dock at the Hartman family cottage at BHL. I can feel that coming. The wood of the deck under my hands. The thermostat showing maybe seventy degrees. I can hear the sound of the water lapping against the dock.

That's my chemo finish line. That spot. It's the spot when I was Natalie's age I would spend who knows how long washing off the dock to grandpa's approval. And a little older getting a bucket of small rocks and hitting them with a whiffle ball bat into the lake imagining I was Kirk Gibson playing for the Tigers in the World Series. Over the raft was a home run.

If all goes well I'll be walking down that dock on Tuesday night the 8th of July. It's coming. I can feel it. And when it does we'll have our moment and thank God for bringing us safely through this part of the journey.

Thank you for walking with us on this journey. Your kindness, prayers, love, and friendship have made this manageable. My wife is amazing. I knew that before all this just couldnt comprehend the depth of it.

From today's Proverbs 2:7-9

"He has success in store for the upright, is the shield of those who walk honestly. Guarding the paths of justice, protecting the way of his faithful ones."

June 8
By Dan Klein — June 8, 2014

Thirty days from today is when Round #12 begins. We're

getting there. Vegas was good. No physical or health issues and it was a really nice break. I was out to dinner Thursday night and had pretty much allowed cancer to vacate my thoughts for a good while—probably 30-45 minutes. Which is probably the longest stretch of time I've gone since day one without some type of reminder, usually physical, that cancer is on. It's 24-7.

It's the hardest part of this. And it is what I have come to appreciate as the biggest difference between being the patient and being anyone else. You can never drop it. Not even for more than a handful of minutes. It's always there. There is always a reminder. Something hurts, something doesn't work right, a look from a stranger that is held a moment past comfortable, it's in the mirror, it's there at my 2:30 AM wake up call and the 5:30 one, too.

So there I am at dinner in Vegas without a thought of cancer, enjoying myself. And then my phone rings. It's the automated call from Vanderbilt with my friendly reminder about my appointment next Wednesday.

Dang cancer. Well played Rumble. You know every trick in the book. Can you just give me an hour? Over the course of five months just one stinking hour? Dang cancer got me on that one.

But boy did I eat in Vegas! Good gravy did I eat. My tastebuds were alive and working. That was freaking awesome.

Filet, pineapple, bacon, croissants with butter and strawberry jam. Forget about the Vegas strip give me the food, baby.

The last several months I've definitely leaned towards

anything with a little kick—salsa, tangy drinks, salty, spicy —you name it I just want to taste something besides the wretched chemo taste. Yuck.

Matthew & Ben loved the wave pool and the white bath robes. It was cute to see those guys fresh out of the tub after a day of swimming sitting in chairs in front of the big windows from the thirty-eighth floor looking out over Vegas in nothing but their bathrobes and slippers. Thinking and laughing, as those two do, about whatever those two think and laugh about.

Those are two special guys. Matthew was my protector. He always walked with me in the airport and sat next to me. "Dad you need me to carry that?" I recognized early on in this journey that I was going to have to accept the fact that I was going from a caregiver to one who is cared for. Someone who you can count on to someone that needs to count on others.

That's not easy. But I didn't have a choice. The decision was made for me and I accepted it. When you see your eight year old son be part of that large committee helping you it's a bit—uncomfortable may be too strong of a word—but I am at least aware of the unnatural order of it. But it's also a life lesson, for both of us, and it's something that makes me proud of him.

Poor Ben, he got caught in a tough spot on the way home. We had a connection in Dallas and got off and found our way to the right gate and set up. Or what we thought was the right gate. Did the usual bathroom and find something to eat. It was about twenty minutes to scheduled departure and Claire mentioned we should be boarding soon.

Yeah, you're right I wonder why we haven't boarded yet?? We found out pretty quickly we were at the wrong gate. So we scrambled, and I don't scramble well these days, to get to the correct gate. And the correct gate was a big escalator ride, a tram ride, and a short dash away.

So Claire and Ben lead the way and Matthew, of course, is hanging back with me. Matthew and I get to the top of the escalator where the platform for the tram is and Claire and Ben are heading back. "What's up??" I ask.

"Got to go back down" Claire says. Just then an airport worker tells Claire she was going the right way and that we need to go to the tram. Claire stops short of the down escalator but Ben just stepped on it with a carryon bag.

And there goes Ben. Drifting lower. "Come on Ben!"

The tram isn't coming yet so we're ok. He's working hard to step up and pull up the carryon bag. And step up and pull up the carryon bag. But he's losing ground. Fast. And it's a long escalator.

"Its ok Ben, just ride down and ride it back up." About halfway back up of course the tram starts to come. Now we're in trouble. He's trying to hustle up but the bag is about half as big as he is. We finally get him and the bag up, get to the tram, and get to our gate without a lot of time to spare. Whew!

That is something that maybe 6 months ago I get frustrated with Ben because the situation is stressful and kids can make for easy outlets for adult's frustrations. But not this time. It certainly wasn't his fault and he was doing everything he could. It was more like an old Laurel and Hardy film with him trying to fight the escalator.

Sometimes things just happen in life and you just have to smile and move on.

Physically—I'm tired. My body is weary of getting poisoned every two weeks

But I've learned that exhaustion is something that more times than not you can push your body through. I have frequent discussions with my body that remind me of getting pre-teen boys out of bed on Sunday mornings.

"Come on, let's go."

"Do we have to?"

"Yup, time to go."

"Just five more minutes."

"Nope, it's time and regardless if you like it or not we're doing this so you might as well make the best of it."

"Ugh, ok."

My finger tips are still an issue. Maybe more of an irritant than an issue. Buttons I'm finding are becoming more difficult. I don't dare reach into the ice box to grab ice—I made that mistake once. I keep looking at my fingers expecting to see little cuts on them to explain the feelings there but they aren't there. Just nerves. Nerves I hope and pray return to normal when my body is done getting pummeled by chemo.

My handwriting is sloppy—sloppier I should say. I've kept a journal for several years. I write in it on a fairly regular basis. Not every day but I try to do several times a week.

I brought it with me to Vegas and as I opened it I opened close to January 13th—the day all this fun began. I have yet to look back in my journal since that day.

But I did go to January 13th and just read the first line "I believe I was told I have cancer today." That was a tough day. And a tougher night. Someday I'll go back and read my entries from that week and the times since then. It will be interesting to get back inside my head and see what was going on. Right now it's just about today and there will be time to look back later.

I've got two and a half more days before the bell rings for Round 10. Hoping to get in a four mile walk tomorrow and a five mile walk Tuesday. I'll have that discussion with my body and it will do, I have found, whatever my head tells it to do. We'll check back in on Wednesday.

Reflections From the End of the Dock:
The Accountability Multiplier

You create a special energy when you reach out and stake a claim to something. A formal "I got this" declaration. Some future event you want to see happen or goal you set out to accomplish which lays somewhere beyond comfortable. Being able to visualize that event. That success. The entire process of intentionally placing that stake in the ground, working towards it, and eventually seeing it come to fruition. One step at a time. So, in the same spirit as my vision board, I booked that trip to Vegas.

Back in April, clean PET scan behind us, clicking submit and booking our flights was the final pounding to firmly set that stake in place. Knowing when I stepped on that plane I would be so close to the finish line for chemo. Knowing I would have to do whatever I could to be able to make that trip. Deliberately creating that special energy. Something to not only look forward to but to work towards.

On top of that special energy there's a magical thing that happens when you share what is important to you with someone else. If you share something that you want to accomplish. By sharing, a probability multiplier occurs that allows that special energy to convert to almost a mystical power. It's one thing to think about it and commit to yourself and quietly place that stake out there. But it's an entirely different animal when you bring someone else into the loop, lay out your plans, and ask not only for their scrutiny but for them to hold you accountable to seeing it through. It creates a degree of healthy vulnerability as well as accountability. And when you can put some form, some structure around that process, good things happen.

I always look forward to my monthly accountability meeting. In hindsight, I don't think our foursome came together by chance. Chris, Mike, Nick, and I all bring something different to the table. We've known each other for years but more as acquaintances than close friends. Our paths would cross casually through various activities but it wasn't until we started meeting for our couples group and then later our men's breakfast that deeper friendships took hold.

Enough similarities for synergy yet enough differences to learn and grow from each other. We all benefit from each other's strengths and perspectives. It's interesting how just in our spiritual and personal life there are timeless principles to living a good life, so it is in business. Certain principles, regardless of the situation, stand: integrity, vision, and work ethic.

There are no substitutes for those. No short cuts. Input equals output. If I put in average effort into my work I should expect average results. So true for all aspects of our lives, be it professional, personal, or spiritual.

If I put in average effort into being a father, if I just get by and do what I think fathers are supposed to do based on what I see in the world today, I should expect to have average relationships with my kids. Average effort into my relationship with Claire equals average marriage. Same thing as a friend.

Why should I expect to get more out of something than what I put in? I think sometimes people think the concept of compounding interest, where small amounts in over a very long period of time equals a large amount out, applies to everything. The five hour work week. Build a million dollar real estate empire with no money down. Lose weight and still eat what you want. Maybe those concepts sell books or seminars. Maybe they work for some people. But they don't work for me. They're missing a critical piece for me.

There's something about pouring everything you have into something that makes seeing it come to fruition that much more meaningful. There's something about going to bed exhausted knowing you gave this day everything you had. Be it a professional goal, the richness of a personal relationship, or your spiritual life. I've learned not to despise but to appreciate the discipline required. I recognize and appreciate the cost of the effort. The grind.

The great thing about sitting down with those guys every month is it provides a structure of review, reflection, and support for what is truly important. Continually reviewing and tracking. It's three hours around a table of updating and challenging. Of sharing successes and struggles. Of probing and questioning. Of laughing and honesty. Of re-energizing and recalibrating.

When we first started it was primarily focused on our professional lives. But we quickly realized through our conversations the first couple of months that our personal and spiritual lives were more important. So we divided it into three distinct sections —spiritual, personal, and professional. Purposefully placed in that order.

It is a consistent process to make sure not only that we have well thought out plans but, more importantly, that those plans are aligned with our values and priorities. Not just a wandering through life. Ultimately arriving at some random place. Rather, purposeful thought and consideration to not only what is really important, but equally important the manner we go about it. And ultimately, where am I trying to go? What am I trying to accomplish? If I do actually achieve these things in this manner is that really where I want to be? Is that the journey and the destination I want? Is that the path I believe God has laid out for me?

At the center of what we do is the distinction between what we have control over and what we don't. The Serenity Prayer. We're not going to spend time and energy on something we can't control. That's a waste of resources. But the parts we do control, especially the ones we have complete control over, we make sure we do our part.

Boy was that ever useful training for life with cancer. It's so easy to get overwhelmed when confronted with a challenge of that magnitude. But I think regardless of the challenge and its magnitude—be it cancer or otherwise—it's still the same approach.

After the initial overwhelming shock wears off and you regain some sort of footing you begin to take inventory. You start to sort through the various pieces of the whole. Dividing them into stacks. Manageable stacks. This stack I can't do a darn thing about so I'm going to do my best not to give those an ounce of my energy. This stack I have some control over and I need to be aware of those and do my part.

But this stack, this is mine. This stack is completely on me. My responsibility. My focus. Everything I got is going here. What a relief. I don't have to get my hands around this larger than life problem called cancer. I don't have to deal with all the different pieces. I know if I allowed myself to do that it would just compound the problem. Through all of the potential complications and factors and things that can and will go wrong my assignment is easy. Just focus on what I control. Just a fraction of the whole. That's my assignment. I'm not a helpless patient. I can and will do my part. That, I can do. That's all I can do.

Round 10

**Too many times we stand aside
And watch the waters slip away
Til we put off til tomorrow
has now become today...**

First song out of chemo
By Dan Klein — June 11, 2014

"The River" by Garth Brooks

You got to love Garth Brooks. It was tempting to pick Garth's "I'm much too young to feel this damn old."

Ding ding. Round 10 has begun. The cumulative effect of chemo is leaning on me. I'm definitely feeling some effects as soon as it gets pumped in. Oh, that horrible chemo taste is pretty much immediately. I won't miss that.

A little curveball today with my treatment. I'll let that cute girl sitting next to me post that later. Crossing the KY/TN state line and home bound. Chemo hole I'm heading your way shortly.

The Curve Ball
By Claire Klein — June 11, 2014

The standard drug regimen for Hodgkin's is ABVD. The B being Bleomycin. When we first started chemo, they told us about Bleomycin toxicity. Apparently, this can cause permanent scarring in one's lungs. Usually, a cough will develop and we were told to be aware of any signs of shortness of breath. In younger patients (yes, Dan, that means you!), they can prescribe high doses of steroids and this usually will take care of it.

Dan has had a dry cough for at least a month or more. We always discuss these things with Dr. Morgan and Leslie. Because it hasn't been accompanied by shortness of breath, they weren't too concerned. And having a negative PET doesn't concern them about the actual lymphoma in his chest. But because it is still lingering they wanted to do a PFT (pulmonary function test). They were able to fit us in early. Otherwise, we would have gone back in the morning for chemo. All of Dan's lung functions look better than initially, when the mass was in his chest. They were looking for one specific level that isn't on his initial PFT that was performed here in Bowling Green. This level was low today, but they have nothing to compare it to. So I will call Graves Gilbert in the morning to see if maybe it was left off the report.

To be on the safe side, they decided to delete Bleomycin today. Dr. Morgan recommends deleting it the last two treatments also. They feel that Bleomycin isn't the most important of the four drugs, the PET is negative, and three weeks of radiation will be more than enough to be successful for a CURE.

I am in awe of Dan. He doesn't get enough sleep, but he gets out of bed every day and sits in his silent classroom. He tries to get to go to work for a few hours and sometimes makes it all day. Otherwise, he is in his office here working. He gets a little horizontal rest, but it isn't easy around here.

Especially, when his littlest princess needs her daddy. We all play wiffleball or kickball in the backyard, and he tries to keep up with the best of us. Dan may feel terrible but he doesn't miss a game (between hockey and baseball, we have had many).

Most importantly, these kids feel loved. Not a night goes by that Dan isn't helping tuck them in and giving them snuggles. Ten down and two to go!

Update
By Claire Klein — June 17, 2014

Good evening to all! After a couple of calls and some persistence, we discovered that Graves Gilbert had the levels that Vandy needed. Dan doesn't really present as having Bleomycin toxicity but his levels do.

Unfortunately, he is now on a mega dose of steroids. We are not very excited about the side effects of steroids, but they definitely outweigh pulmonary fibrosis. We know that all of Dan's past softball teams will be calling him to play or pinch hit. And these steroids are legal!

Your continued thoughts and prayers are appreciated!!

Note from Claire

As Dan began to have another lingering cough, it was difficult at times not to become preoccupied with the cause. Would we be in a state of constant worry every time he gets a cough? The threat of Blcomycin toxicity and resultant scarring of the lungs. Man, it's bad enough to have cancer but then you have to suffer all these other terrible side effects. Reminders of this horrific disease that just won't let you forget. I didn't know the extent of what this scarring of the lungs would do, but I would get this image of a maturing Dan on oxygen years down the road.

Maybe it is just me being me, but as a healthcare worker, I find that I am a little more practical in my thinking than some. The specific results of Dan's initial lung test(performed in Bowling Green) were not in Vandy's records. My brain started working in overdrive. If the protocol for Hodgkin's is the same everywhere, then those results should be at our local clinic. He had that test run there prior to us deciding to be treated at Vandy. If they did indicate toxicity, then Dan needed to be on steroids as well as having Bleomycin taken out of his chemo regimen. Due to it being late in the day, we called the next morning which was a Thursday. Yes, they had the results. They told him that he could pick them up on Monday. That is when the practical healthcare worker in me took charge! All they needed to do was a few clicks on the computer and push print. I told Dan, "You call there and tell them that you might have Bleomycin toxicity and you need to know now! You tell them that you cannot wait until Monday to be put on steroids. You need to know now!" And an hour later, Dan is driving to the clinic for his results. He makes his call to Leslie at Vandy and a few hours later he is taking his steroids. This all really frustrates me. What about the people out there who just go along with the protocol? What about the people who don't have anyone fighting for them?

Early on our friend, Cravens, shared with me some of the things that helped him while his wife battled breast cancer.

He focused on Luke 8:50: "Fear is Useless, What Is needed Is Trust."

Was I scared? Of course, I was scared. I was selfishly scared for myself. I was scared that our children would grow up without their daddy. I could have gotten preoccupied by all my fears, so I told myself that I had to focus on today and trust that we would get through this time of uncertainty. I knew that was how Dan was getting through his battle, I would do the same. There were days when my mind would drift to the unknown. The fear would start to creep back in, and I would have to remind myself to refocus on today. And now, I try not to linger too long on the possibilities of a return. I begin to ponder the terrible side effects that come with chemo and radiation that can occur down the road. I feel some apprehension when Dan gets a cough. I watch his symptoms closely making sure that it is a productive cough or one that accompanies a cold.

And I occasionally have to go back to my mantra, Luke 8:50: "Fear is Useless, What is Needed is Trust."

Strong Week*
By Dan Klein — June 18, 2014

Greetings from the official start of Strong Week* Caring-bridge Nation. I will say despite the whole bleomycin toxicity body blow (what's a little chemo poisoning after all?) I feel pretty darn good. Knock on wood I would say it's as good as I have felt in sometime.

I had some hesitations about the level of steroids and I just stopped reading the side effect page(s) and am just enjoying the main effect—which is I feel pretty darn good and it was a soft visit to the chemo hole to boot.

Eating like a horse and enjoying every moment of it. Sleeping like a baby—sleep an hour, cry an hour, repeat all night long—not really that bad.

I made it to work full days all this week. I have no idea what I did (kidding). I was back out walking about thirty minutes Monday and then got a good forty-five minute walk in Tuesday. Not sure about today though. It's hot and the sun is out.

Which brings me to one of those things in life you never consider until you are in some odd combination of circumstances and are faced with it. That is I'm supposed to avoid exposure to sunlight while on the steroids—or maybe it's the other drug I'm suppose to take on Mondays and Thursdays to counter the steroids. Or maybe it's the other one to offset that one. I can't keep up.

Now I think technically it is "prolonged sunlight" and that seems a bit subjective. And I stopped reading about it so I don't really know to be honest. So I'm playing this little game of "avoid the sunlight." Which is half amusing and half frustrating because it's really hard to avoid sunlight.

But it's kind of fun and I'd encourage you to give it a try for a day. A full day to get the full effect. Let me know if you have any success because I haven't figured it out yet. Even in the car it's hard to avoid sunlight.

So I have this pain in my lower right ribs. If we're reaching for silver linings it makes some of the others problems move to the back while this one takes its turn in the driver's seat. When I breathe in deeply I get that tickle in the chest and then a cough. Or if I cough, sneeze, or laugh it feels like someone is jabbing me in that spot with a fork. Not too bad but it's there.

I don't know how long it takes for us to know if the steroids are working but I can say it is not getting any better and if anything has gotten worse over the last week. I would assume it takes some time so we'll check in with Leslie and David at Vandy next week and hopefully get good news.

The concern is that bleomycin can cause long term or permanent lung damage. Or worse and we won't go there. Part of what lays in the back of my mind as a big picture concern for this chapter of my life is I don't get to close it completely. I end up with some health issue that stays with me and potentially has an impact on my standard of living and activity level going forward.

I'm hoping that based on the fact that apparently my level of symptoms compared to my level of complaining about the symptoms don't seem to match the levels of the test may indicate this baby will just go away. That would be based on my logic of medicine which really has no basis.

But I like it and I'm going with it.

We'll see and I would ask for your prayers on that one. I'll deal with whatever the outcome is but I have been putting a lot of hope into getting my body and life back to normal in the next sixty to ninety days and I'd rather not have to back up and adjust my expectations.

Speaking of getting my body and life back together for the first time I am looking forward to chemo next week! There's a string of words I never thought I'd put together. We're this close. Let's go and get it over with.

Last chemo is scheduled for Monday, July 7th. Our plan is to head to Nashville & knock out chemo and then the fun begins. We'll head out of Vandy and post the final first song out of chemo, pick up kids in BG, and head 672 miles straight north to Beautiful Higgins Lake (BHL).

Yes that is crazy and, frankly, I have no idea if it will work. Honestly I'm pretty certain it won't.

Claire is going along with it but I know what she is thinking. But I have a moment on the end of that dock waiting for me and I will be there, good Lord willing, Tuesday night before the sun sets. That gives us thirty hours, give or take. Surely we can do that. Right Dear?

I'll spend my last trip into the chemo hole at that sacred of places in the Hartman family surrounded by my family. I'll sit in the chair at the kitchen table that my grandfather would sit in and watch the sun rise over that beautiful piece of God's creation.

I'll think of him and his battle with cancer that took him much too soon. And I'll sort through my feelings of incredible compassion and a new found perspective on how the heck he must have felt going through cancer treatment in the 1970's. Good gravy what was that like?? It's all I can do to handle it as someone who is in the prime of their life (Funny, I think I've always thought I was living in the prime of my life. Hope I always do.) and with all the advancements in medicine.

I just want to hold him and tell him I'm so sorry for what he had to endure. I just can't imagine what that must have been like. I'm very much aware there's a debt to be paid for all those cancer patients before me who, willingly or not, played a role in the great experiment of treating and curing this dreaded disease to get us to the point where we are today.

I'll start with Grandpa Hartman.

To wrap I am hoping and praying this whole lung thing gets resolved and in the near term it doesn't throw off the chemo schedule. I don't think it will. Same holds for radiation which is set to begin July 14th and end—insert great big "alleluia!"—on Friday, August 9th.

On Saturday August 10th Claire, John, and I are stepping on a plane and heading to San Diego.

That's my next mark after BHL—stepping over the threshold from the gangway onto the airplane knowing chemo and radiation is behind me. I may be glowing but I will be done!

Reflections From the End of the Dock: Theoretical vs Real Life Questions

---

Would I run into a burning building to save my wife? Would I trade places with my child who got dealt the cancer card? Would I stand up for my faith and not deny Jesus in the face of persecution? Those are all easy theoretical questions to answer—of course. I would absolutely lay down my life for who and what is most important to me.

Those are easy to answer partially because there's no way to prove it. There's never, or extremely rarely, a chance to validate the response. But there are more difficult questions to answer. More difficult because they are daily and there is opportunity for immediate validation.

Will I make sure I leave work early so Claire can join her friends for book club tonight? Will I put aside what I want to do on Saturday morning to not only devote the time to doing what the kids want to do but to be fully present and engaged when we are doing it? Will I make it a habit of getting out of bed twenty minutes earlier than I'd like to and spend time in the scriptures and the classroom of silence?

Can I answer the bell without thinking when it comes to the big ones? Sure I can. But can I answer the bell on a daily basis for the little ones?

In theory it seems so easy. But in reality it can be much more difficult. If I don't have to give up my life, actually die in a burning building or take on cancer, the least I can do is devote a little time each day to those same people I say I would give everything to. Maybe those small things are somewhat trivial in and of themselves. But start stringing them together on a consistent and daily basis and you have your habits. String those habits together and you have your life.

Through cancer certainly, but before as well, I have been given so much by so many. All of the small daily sacrifices that were done for my benefit. Some I received as the primary beneficiary. Done intentionally for my benefit like a home cooked meal during chemo. Other sacrifices by my parents, grandparents, and beyond, I was a contingent beneficiary, like Grandpa's cancer treatment.

Not the theoretical extremes that we can confidently commit ourselves to but the everyday simple acts of giving of ourselves for someone else. Those demand immediate payment. All I can do is try to pay that forward and slowly chip away at it knowing there's not an amortization schedule long enough to reach maturity. Part of my payment schedule is to pay back in kind. A meal or a yard mowed to someone who is unable. A prayer or note to someone who is struggling.

But another part of my payment schedule is to go for it. To not just live but live a life of meaning and purpose. Lean in and take in all that life offers. Celebrate the successes of all sizes. Realize that whatever failures may come were achieved through participation and effort, from being in the arena, and not absentia. To not just live for myself but live a life of those daily deaths for others and by doing so living a life laid out in gospels.

I've been given the chance. I've been granted the perspective.

I have the awareness that no matter what issues I think I have to deal with, someone is coming to grips that their life is coming to an end. Their life, their chance, is transitioning from present tense to past tense. I have the awareness that no matter what I'm struggling with today someone is sitting in the chemotherapy waiting room for the first time. Not knowing how the poison will affect them or if it will even work.

I have the gift of being on a ninety day check out from the cancer center. That keeps you humble. That keeps you grateful. That keeps you hungry for living life every day.

"So don't you sit upon the shoreline
and say you're satisfied.
Choose to chance the rapids
and dare to dance the tide"

Round 11

**If you stand before the power of hell
and death is at your side...**

First song out of chemo
By Dan Klein — June 25, 2014

"Be Not Afraid" by Father Robert J. Dufford

"You shall cross the barren dessert
but you shall not die of thirst.
You shall wander far in safety
though you do not know the way.
You shall speak your words to foreign men
and they will understand.
You shall see the face of God and live.
If you past the raging waters
in the sea you shall not drown.
If you walk amid the burning flames
you shall not be harmed.
If you stand before the power of hell and death is at
your side know that I am with you through it all.
Be not afraid. I go before you always.
Come follow me and I will give you rest."

I've always liked that song, but boy does it have a bit more meaning these days.

We have a little more baggage with us this round. Ben joined us. Ben had an ear appointment so Claire worked that into the schedule. And it saves her yet another trip to Vandy. Oh, if she only knew what she was getting herself into.

So not only do I have a cute girl next to me, I got a cute boy behind me. Which is nice. Because they're cute. And sweet.

The Rumble is not done. I can feel that. Im thankful for

this last round being as easy as it was. Im not sure if I missed a day of work the last two weeks. Darn near felt normal. If you would have told me four months ago I would have felt this good come the end of June I would have said you were crazy. Bracing for impact and ramping up for the final push.

And the hair is still hanging in there—sort of. Still the thin, patchy, tennis ball fuzzy look but it's there. I actually thought it may have been coming back in the other day when I paid attention to it. But then I got in better light. Nope. Still going. Still have in my orange afro request for the grow back phase.

Our usual dynamic duo team of David and Leslie were out today so we visited with a new person. Still keeping an eye on the lung situation. It's better but still there. The next move is to ratchet down the steroids and then see what the next scan has to say. That scan is July 16th and it is a big day. Last scan in April was clean and we expect this one to be clean as well. If not something has veered off track.

There'll be some anxious moments waiting for the results. We'll stop in the chapel between the scan and heading to see Leslie and David for the results. We'll get into the exam room and chat and wait to hear the clickity clack of Leslie's shoes coming down the hall. Faster pace followed by quick swinging door and smiling face poking in is good. Group hug and we can check that milestone off and are one step closer to remission (two years) and eventually cure (five years).

Slow pace, pause, shadows under the door not so good.

As we start to wind down this part of the treatment phase

I'm very aware that I have been somewhat shielded from the full assault and brunt of the effects of chemotherapy. It's been no picnic but it could have been a lot worse. A lot worse. I see that in the people who get wheeled into the chemo waiting room and am grateful that it hasn't been worse than it has been.

Thank you Lord. Thank you Claire and family and friends for always providing the right card, post, package, visit, comments just when it was needed most. And thank you to good medicine.

It's very comforting to know He goes before me into the ring. I'm following blindly. And I'm definitely looking forward to some rest.

Ding ding. Here comes #11.

Final push of chemo
By Dan Klein — July 5, 2014

Its July. Thank God its July!

Special greetings to all the Hartman clan gathering up at BHL today at the Pride of Earl G Hartmans. I am with you in spirit and will be there shortly. Thanks to Ryan and Aunt Mary & Nana for driving 500+ miles each yesterday. They met in Indianapolis with John and Matthew so they could get up there for the reunion. Sounds like a good time was had by all at Uncle Doug's last night.

All is well here. Just the usual chemo cycle stuff. For some reason I'm trying to convince myself that since Monday is the last round of chemo I should start to be feeling better already. My body does a pretty good job of reminding me that we're not done just yet. The Rumble can flex its muscles whenever it wants to remind me of who is in charge.

Just one more trip to the chemo hole. Just one more.

I have yet to be able to respond adequately when asked what chemo is like. I dont have words to capture it and do it justice. I would say everyone who goes through it reacts differently to it and there are different cocktails depending on what monster you are trying to eliminate. It's something that in conversations with others who have gone through chemo there's just no need to explain. It's just a lousy place to visit and I'm looking forward to checking out of there permanently.

The cycles for me have been consistently inconsistent as far as side effects and symptoms. Other than my dear faithful companions—and soon to be dearly departed faithful companions—nausea and fatigue. A little more nausea this go around which is not appreciated. I suppose I should throw in their buddy "horrible mouth" into the mix as well. That little jerk is pretty much a given and constant and begins in earnest even before I get unplugged from the IV, strap on my backpack, and Claire & I make the slow walk down the hall out of the chemo wing. Other than those three old friends it's just a crapshoot as to who is going to show up that cycle.

Generally speaking the first couple of days after chemo are ok. Not good but ok. Then you slide into the hole and it's no fun for a few days. Then it's a week or so of climbing back out of the hole to where you were before you slipped into that dreaded place. And for the last five months that cycle has been repeated on day fifteen. Just as you get back to par the bell rings again and you start all over by design. You give your body all it can handle. Allow it to recover. Then whack it again. That makes sense. I don't like it. But it makes sense and I can appreciate that.

Looking forward to the silencing of that bell. No more ringing. No more rounds. Just silence. Just silence. No sound will have ever sounded so good as that silence. And being able to see what day fifteen and beyond feels like out of chemo. I'm anxious to see how long it takes for me to get back to feeling normal. Today is day ten out of chemo and I say I feel good. That is a qualified "good" and is based on chemo's standard.

But it's coming. The final bell is about to ring and Round 12 with The Rumble is here. That means the end is in sight. Thank you Lord the end is in sight for this part of the journey. When it is all done I will slip as quietly and as quickly out of the ring and get back to the dressing room. Change and slip quietly out that door.

No LeBron James chest beating look-at-me moment. No "In your face!" taunting. I'd be willing to line up to shake hands as they do after the final game of a hard fought NHL playoff series but would gladly pass on that as well. I don't dare even look The Rumble in the eye let alone taunt it. No way. I know what it is capable of. I see it every other week in the chemo waiting room. And that's not even the inpatient chemo waiting room or, heaven forbid, the children's cancer center. I don't dare go there.

Just let me move on. Please Lord let me move on and go back to my little boring life with my family and friends. Just the quiet satisfaction of being done. Facing a task and moving through it. I know if The Rumble ever demands a rematch it will get one and I don't want any part of that. I don't want any part of that.

So we wrap up chemo Monday and then the next item on the agenda is scan #2. That's on July 16th before radiation begins July 21st. Scan #1 in April was as clean as it could be and another clean scan is the next step in the process.

I look forward to posting the final "First song out of chemo" Monday afternoon as we head north. I've known for some time what that song is going to be.

Reflections From the End of the Dock:
The Most Important Day of My Life

Going through cancer as a young father and husband you are forced to face some harsh realities. To say facing a premature death with your loving wife and four young children next to you is disheartening is like saying the Arctic Circle can be a little chilly in winter. But, I have discovered, there are worse things than dying too young. Believe it or not there are worse conditions to find yourself in than coming to the solemn understanding that you are reaching the point where it's time to say your goodbyes much sooner than you ever thought possible.

Worse than dying too young is dying with regret. Knowing you were given the chances. Knowing you were presented with the opportunities. But, for whatever reason, you didn't make the most of them. Or didn't even make the attempt. Maybe you lived an ok life or even a good life. But you kept putting off until tomorrow. Believing for some reason tomorrow would be a better time than today. And then, all of a sudden, it's too late. When tomorrow does finally arrive those chances and opportunities are gone. Or you run out of tomorrows. Tomorrow becomes today. Then, before you know it, it becomes yesterday.

But there is a slot reserved at the top of that horrible list for a condition even worse than dying too young. Even worse than dying with regret. Yes, there is something worse than dying too young or dying with regret. More painful and disheartening than those is one far more difficult to come to grips with. The condition in life you never want to find yourself in is *living* with regret.

Knowing that on some random day the quality of life you knew, a life full of a capabilities and opportunities, can be snatched away. Leaving you with something less in its place. A shell of that life that you once knew. A mere shadow of your previous existence. Replaced with a life of discomfort. A life of limitations. A life of regret. Gone in a heartbeat. Gone with one cough.

Why didn't I do that when I had the chance? What was I afraid of? If I only had the chance to do it over again what would I do? What couldn't I do?

I appreciated life more than most before that cough. I knew what I had was special. I didn't need cancer to stamp an exclamation point on that for me. I'm glad when I was forced to sort through life's regret process it was fairly easy. But easy as it was it was still painful. I couldn't imagine having to wade through real regret. Going through all the "I wish I would haves."

I think most cancer survivors will tell you they don't take much for granted in this life. Having gone through all those layers of pain and discomfort. Having stood before the power of hell and to know with absolute certainty that death is by your side. Having to go through the potentially painful process of sorting out feelings of regret for what you let pass you by. It's easy to appreciate the gift of everyday.

Or let me correct that and say, at least for me, it's easier. Still not always easy. For even after going through all that cancer demands I still find myself at times wanting to settle. Finding it comfortable to yield to apathy and default to putting off til tomorrow. The fear of failure and the cost of discipline are real. But as powerful as those can be, I know the pain of regret is greater. Much greater. The pain of regret makes them look insignificant.

I've come up with my own equation for life. A mathematical sentence that captures the gift of cancer:

$$(FofF + CofD)^2 < PofR$$

It reads simply: The fear of failure plus the cost of discipline is exponentially less than the pain of regret. It's my formula for life. It's the gift that cancer has granted me, spoken in the language of math.

No matter how great the apprehension of trying something and failing and no matter how much effort required to see it through, I know if I don't do it someday the regret will be so much more. And if I don't at least try and give it my all there will eventually come a time when I won't be able to do a darn thing about it. The chances and opportunities of this life will have passed me by.

Those things you always said you'd do someday. Things you'll get around to. Eventually. Down the road. Tomorrow. Start your own business. Set out on that long road trip out West. Finish a marathon. Learn how to play the guitar. Live every day a life laid out in the gospels.

I'm embarrassed to admit, even with all that I have gone through and experienced, that I still struggle with those tendencies. But the gift of cancer is that when I start struggling with those, I have a quick reboot to gratefulness and awareness of the power of right now. Knowing that as long as I trust and allow myself to be guided and to use the gifts and experiences He has so graciously granted I will always be on the right path. And with it the realization that out of all of the days of my life, however many or however few I may have in front of me, the most important one is always the same. Today. This day is the day that matters. This day is the most important day of my life.

"...know that I am with you, through it all.
Be not afraid..."

Round 12

**The smile on your face
lets me know that you need me.
There's a truth in your eyes
saying you'll never leave me....**

Final (and last!) song out of chemo
By Dan Klein — July 7, 2014

"When you say nothing at all" by Alison Krauss

This one is for that cute girl who has had the worst seat on this bus. Much worse than mine for sure. It's the song we danced to for the first time as husband and wife. Just after taking our vows of "I promise to be true to you in good times and bad, in sickness and in health. . . ." Who would have thunked it.

Claire and I have our own little nonverbal language of sorts. Never set out to create it. I suppose most married people acquire that over the years. The first few days, as we sorted our way through this, we "talked" more by not talking. It's nice to be in tune with someone to the point where a look or a nudge a certain way is all that is needed to say what you need to say.

Long day at Vandy today. Cancer centers aren't immune to holiday weekend logistics. Sitting in the chemo waiting room has become for me this unique observation post. I guess the gift of cancer offered me the opportunity for some bonus time to let it all soak in one last time. But we're finally out for the chemo finish line. Stuck in rush hour traffic in Nashville and much later than we had hoped but who the heck cares.

I don't know how, when, or what the gesture of adequately being able to express our appreciation to everyone looks like but please start by celebrating this day and moment with us and knowing we would not have made it without you. Northbound—at last!

Strong Week

By Dan Klein — July 14, 2014

We are one week out of the last chemo and all is well and right with the world. I would say my final—and hopefully my last ever trip to the chemo hole—was probably the easiest one. That's a pleasant surprise. I know being with the family had a lot to do with it and knowing chemo is behind us. Even though Uncle Don said how much I looked like Grandma Klein.

We had a great trip to Michigan and BHL. I enjoyed reaching my chemo finish line at the end of the dock. Ahh:) They had a "Happy End of Chemo to You" cake complete with singing. Thanks guys that was really nice.

Back to Vandy tomorrow and then again Wednesday to gear up for radiation that I think will begin next Monday. We were supposed to go Wed for the PET but our friends at Anthem have informed us they will not cover it. Great. So instead, we are scheduled for a CT scan tomorrow and then back to meet with David & Leslie Wednesday for results.

Summary—CT scan tomorrow, results Wed, radiation to begin Monday.

Feeling good. Sleeping better. Pain in the side is not going away and comes and goes—but mostly comes. I'm afraid that sucker may just hang around and is going to be an issue, but we'll deal with that.

My hair, I think, is actually getting darker. Still waiting on the orange afro to start coming in.

I stepped on the scale last night and haven't weighed this much in probably ten years. Go figure. I know the steroids have a role in that (only five more days) but I also think I'm just eating more after experiencing "horrible mouth" for so darn long. When I can eat and not feel bad and actually taste what I'm eating instead of that terrible chemo taste I just eat. And eat and eat and eat. Boy do things taste good these days. The whole "you don't appreciate something fully until it's taken away" thing. Did I mention I like to eat these days??

Thank you for the prayers and continued and constant support. Clean scan this week is what we're praying and looking for. Will update Wednesday.

I'm heading for the cream!

Reflections From the End of the Dock:
Claire

I finally made it. We, finally made it. The end of the dock. The finish line of chemo. Sitting at that spot, Natalie next to me, processing what the last 6 months were and reflecting on the lessons learned. The coolness of the northern water on my feet. Listening to the gentle lapping of the waves against the dock. It was exactly as I envisioned it back on those cold dark days of February when I needed something to hang on to. This moment was what I had been working towards and this moment was what I used to create energy and motivation when things got really tough and cancer was too much. Sitting there feeling the overwhelming sense of relief that chemo was done and beginning to mentally unwrap the gift of cancer.

As promised, I thanked God for bringing me to that spot. Knowing He was there waiting for me but that He was also always with us. I brought with me in spirit our family and friends to the end of the dock.

They had done so much for us, I thought, through their acts of kindness and love. I was humbled and embarrassed at needing every ounce of it.

I was thankful I didn't have to bring Claire with me in spirit because, as always, she was there. Standing behind us on the beach.

There's an old riddle that captures the essence of Claire:

You are driving along in your
car on a wild, stormy night, it's raining
heavily when suddenly you pass by a bus
stop.

Leslie and I have this friendly debate with Claire and Cravens about who drew the short end of the stick going through cancer with young children? The patient or the caregiver/spouse/ parent?

You see three people waiting for a bus:
An old lady who looks as if she is about to die.
An old friend who once saved your life.
The perfect partner you have been dreaming about.

Leslie and I know it's the caregiver. Claire and Cravens shake their heads in protest and laugh. But we know we're right. We know it's not even close. With very little exception everybody will be handed the challenge, at some stage of their life, to play one of those two roles. Either the one in need of care or the one called on to provide care.

Which one would you choose to offer a ride
to, knowing very well that there could only
be one passenger in your car?

As the patient, my role is simple. Get through the next proce-dure. Get through the next treatment. Get through the next day. Please Lord, get me through the night. As the patient you have no choice. You can't opt out. But the caregiver does have a choice. And it's not just the choice to carry this incredible weight forced upon them—most will execute their required duty. But so incredibly important to the patient is the manner in which they do so.

You pull over, give the car keys to your
old friend and have them drive the old lady
to the hospital.
You stand with your perfect partner and
face the storm.

She never flinched. She never ducked for cover. When you stand next to that level of grace there is no trial too big. We stood at that horrible bus stop called cancer and rode that storm out. Together.

"The touch of your hand says
you'll catch me if ever I fall.
You say it best when
you say nothing at all."

After the Rumble

Clean Scan #2
By Claire Klein — July 16, 2014

Good news...Dan's CT scan was clean. We are over another hurdle. It was a long day at Vandy but easy to endure, when you are handed good news! We met with the radiation oncologist and are beginning the plans to start treatment.

Thank you for keeping us in your thoughts and prayers! We are on our way home, and he feels well enough to be the cute driver today! :)

Note from Claire

One night, probably three to four treatments in, we were upstairs tucking in the kids for the night. We had moved our bedroom upstairs to the Man Cave Recovery Room and the four kids were sleeping together across the hall. I noticed that Dan was absent from the kids' room. I walked out and found him sitting on the top step, hunched over with his arms on his knees, and his forehead on his arms. It was a moment of "How in the world did we get to this place?" I sat down next to him and threw my arm around his shoulders. I assured him that it would be ok. I would be with him all the way.

I sat and thought about all the times that I have heard people talk about friends or family that have had cancer. They say, he/she has never asked why this has happened to them. I wondered why not ask why?? If you live a healthy lifestyle as Dan had, why not ask why? My husband who was 6'5' and 185 and exercised regularly. He was going to boot camp and eating nuts and protein bars. If he wasn't going to ask why then I was.

That's when a little of the anger stage crept into my mind. I've seen it through my patients. How does the 300 pound sedentary person who smokes make it to 40 plus without having cancer? How is this fair? Is it appropriate for me to question. Maybe not. And I know that eventually those leading an unhealthy lifestyle will eventually be handed their share of health problems.

And then there was Dan asking why not him. You cannot ponder on the why very long. It got me nowhere. So we traveled through this journey together as a family, we just lived in the moment. With the final scan before starting radiation set, we felt confident that it would be clean. And when it was clean we were overjoyed. Over the last chemo hurdle and onto radiation. At this point, statistically, we were at an over 90% cure rate. Finally, Dan started to feel good all the time. We could get back to our regular routines without those chemo hangovers.

I recently was a table leader at our yearly church retreat. Taking this role, I knew that I had to get up in front of all the attendees and staff to share my story. I battled for a few months as to whether I could do it. I had attended the year before and knew what it entailed. Each talk was very emotional. Friends and fellow parishioners up at the podium baring their souls. Was I ready for this? This retreat, Koinonia, translating to "community", is only attended one time. To be involved in the future entails helping in the kitchen, being a table leader, or taking on some other type of ancillary role. I knew that Dan was going as an attendee this year. I finally quit dragging my feet and said, YES! At the end of the weekend, one of Dan's accountability friends, Nick, who was also a table leader, was praising my talk. He went on to say how incredible the experience can be and how cool that two years from now my story could be totally different. I like to think that life has gone back to normal but the thought of my story changing is a little daunting. I am not so sure that I want this story to change. I might have had enough change already. So I will just live in the moment and try my hardest not to get too preoccupied regarding how my story will continue.

Day 15
By Dan Klein — July 21, 2014

It's been fifteen days since chemo and I'm enjoying getting that crud out of my system once and for all. I've been waiting and looking forward to my day fifteen. No more going from day fourteen to day one and getting my rear handed to me. Again and again.

Boy how do I say thank you? Everyone going through this should be as blessed as we are to have the kind of support and cheering section that we've experienced. I have no idea. All I have is just inadequate for what we have received. Just know every comment and "like" and note and card and donut and gift card and holy smokes whoever sent that anonymous gift thank you so much—Claire and I have been trying to figure out the proper way to express our appreciation for that and dont know where to start or who to send it to.

Everything is appreciated and will always be remembered.

Feeling good. Feeling really good. Got in my walk today with some running. I've been working on getting my laps at Kereiakes down to fifteen minutes a lap. During chemo I was hovering around seventeen minutes per lap on day eight and could get it close to fifteen minutes by day fourteen. I got in four laps today at fifty-nine minutes and twenty seconds. That's five miles and I feel good about that. I'll try that again tomorrow and then give my legs the day off on Wednesday before picking back up Thursday.

They, my legs, are not so enthusiastic about this whole walking/running thing and getting back in shape. I almost shut it down today after half a lap because my shins were talking to me. Thankfully by the time I made it back around to my car they were quiet and content to keep on going. I remind my shins and calves and quads that this is not a democracy. And while I appreciate their input and I do listen to them—I've learned when you're body talks to you you better listen up—but I make the final call. They understand.

And regardless if I think I can or I think I can't, I know I'm right.

I also made it to Vandy (see below), got to work for a few hours, took the kids to Beech Bend tonight, and played kickball in the backyard after we got home. That's not far from a normal day around the Klein house—and it's a busy day—but it is so nice to be capable.

So the medical stuff: Radiation has been moved back until Thursday, August 14th after we get back from San Diego. The original plan was to get fifteen days of radiation done in three weeks. That didnt allow for any margin of error with our trip three weeks away and the doc thought it would be better to move it until we get back. If something went wrong and we had to miss some days we would possibly have to start all over again.

So we just decided to move it back. I would prefer to get it done and get it over with, but thats ok and its the right decision. The good news is that means I have another three weeks off. I like it!!

We've had three trips to Vandy in the last week. Today was the day I got positioned in the radiation "tube" and had the mold formed under me. No big deal except for the breathing part. The process is I lay down, put my arms over my head and hold onto a metal handle, hold very still, breath normally and then big breath in and hold my breath—for thirty seconds. Thats' a long time—for me anyways. Seconds twenty-five thru thirty got a little interesting. I have also joined the ranks of the tattooed! Sorry Mom. I just wish I had a cooler story and a better tatt. Just three little black dots to line me up for the beam. One on my chest and one on each of my sides. A few more permanent souvenirs. They go along nicely with the other marks on my chest that serve as my morning reminders in the mirror of my time with The Rumble.

Don't worry Mom, I can still donate blood—I asked. I think I'll wait awhile though.

Sleep and hair are good—or at least better and moving in the right direction. All in all things are very good.

I'm looking forward to some time off and working towards 14:45 laps.

Radiation has begun
By Dan Klein — August 15, 2014

The radiation phase of treatment began yesterday and continued today with not much excitement to report - which is the way I like it.

I have a standing 9:00 appointment for the next few weeks mon-fri and I was walking out the door by 9:15 this morning. It is interesting to walk through the department there and see the different molds hanging on the wall. The molds are what they "set" you in when you get on the table so you are in the same position every time.

Because my treatment is in my chest my mold is of my back made in whatever position they told me to get into and "stay very, very still". It hangs on the wall like a snow sled next to the others like it with the owner's name tag hanging from it. Above those hang several molds of heads and shoulders.

The first time I turned the corner and saw those out of the corner of my eye I had to do a double take before putting it all together. A row of white mesh-looking head and shoulders greeting you when you turn the corner. Each representing their owner and their own unique journey with cancer.

Pretty easy process. I check in, wait for Thomas to come get me, lay on the table under this machine and allow them (Thomas and Emily) to get me lined up.

There are little red beams that come from I don't know where and they match up with my little black tattoos and also the "X's" and lines they have written on me. They run back to their little safe spot and talk to me through the intercom "Big breath in and hold..." The maching rumbles while I'm holding my breath and then stops and then I get the "you can breath" call.

I do get the feeling Thomas is new on the job. Yesterday Emily did all the talking but this morning Thomas did the whole "Big breath in..." but when the machine stopped he didnt do the "You can breath." And, being the good patient I try to be, I didnt breath until I heard Emily come on a few seconds later than usual and quickly gave me the nod to breath. We'll have to work on that.

As it was told to me it takes longer to park and walk in than the entire actual radiation process. They have valet parking there which is very nice and we used that for chemo everytime. But I take a little pride in passing that and doing my own parking these days. And another benefit of this phase of treatment is I don't have to go to labs to get blood work done—although I do miss seeing my friend Miss Fannie there at the regsitration desk. "Mmm, mmm child, you sure don't look no 40 years old!" I like Fannie.

So other than having a chest and sides that look like I've let Natalie draw all over me with lines and x's it's pretty much business as usual around the Klein house. I feel good. Food tastes great. And water taste great—that's really nice. Not back to 100% but working on it. Still have a few minor lingering effects from chemo but hopefully they will eventually fade. Working pretty much normally. Got my five miles in today at Kereiakes. I was getting my time down to fifty-three minutes. And I think my side is getting better or at least I havent noticed it in the last few days. That's very good.

We had a great trip to San Diego. Weather was of course perfect and we were able to take in a ballgame among other things. Hair is good and to the point where I think I look pretty much "normal" in that department. I can tell that it is definitely a different texture—not curly but whispy, I might say. It may be a bit lighter also. Just a little different. Which is kind of fun to all of a sudden have a different head of hair. I suppose when you go from having very thin hair to any kind of hair you think it's kind of fun.

Sleep is very good. Im back to being able to fall asleep mid sentence at night and having to actually set the alarm clock now that school is in session. I do enjoy being better rested but I must say I do miss my 4:30-6:30 AM time where it seemed like I had the entire world to myself. But I'll take the sleep.

It's no fun when night time rolls around and you dont look forward to going to sleep. So we keep moving forward. Two sessions of radiation down and sixteen more to go. I believe the last one is scheduled for the Tuesday following Labor Day.

Radiation Update
By Dan Klein — August 26, 2014

We're already halfway through radiation and everything seems to be moving along as expected. The dates got moved around a bit but it is looking like seventeen total doses/sessions with the last one being Monday, September 8th. It's five days a week at Vandy and it's typically in and out very quickly. It was nice to have a couple of friends go along yesterday for the trip—thanks guys.

I appreciate the efficiency of this process. They are usually waiting for me when I come in and within ten minutes I'm walking back out onto the street. I set my stop watch app on my phone as I walk through the doors to the building just for fun and see how long it takes. It's usually ten to twelve minutes. Today I even met with the nurse for vitals and the doctor after that and it was twenty-five minutes between pulling in the parking garage and pulling out. That's pretty impressive. It was eleven minutes in the Panera drive thru afterwards.

Several mornings I pass one of our favorite chemo nurses, Crystal, as I walk out of the building and she is walking in. We high five as we pass each other. You get to know them pretty well and come to understand it takes a special person to work at a cancer center. It's a job to pay the bills but it also is a calling for many of them. Many of them draw the distinction between working inpatient vs.

outpatient cancer centers. The difference being inpatient cancer is mostly terminal.

A pattern seemed to emerge of the nurses that out of college they took traveling jobs that placed them at inpatient hospitals. To our friends in the medical field they know that traveling jobs tend to pay more but you also get placed in positions where there is typically high turnover or for whatever reason an inability to fill or keep positions filled. Inpatient cancer centers seems to be high on that list.

Our radiation doctor said everything seems to be going fine. We like him. He's no David and Leslie and we look forward to seeing them again in a few weeks. He's a very confident man and also short. That combination is not lost on a tall guy.

The only thing he suggested/prescribed at this point is a daily nap. He obviously knows his stuff. My body is tired. Being a chemical dump for who knows what toxic blend for five months and then getting zapped by radiation for three-plus weeks, my body is looking for the finish line. Naps would be good and I'm going to try to take him up on that.

I've backed off the walking and running to just allow my body some time. That finish line is approaching. Thirteen days away is the last scheduled radiation treatment. We wait six weeks or so after that and do the final scan. With the first two being clean it would be a major surprise if scan number three was not. If Hodgkins lymphoma is going to come back the highest probability of recurrence is in the first twelve months. That gives me another moment next 4th of July at BHL to wait and pray for.

Almost Done
By Dan Klein — September 4, 2014

Just two more radiation treatments to go. One tomorrow and then wrapping up on Monday. It's getting a little old driving to Nashville every day. Honestly I think it's just getting old starting my day off being around nurses and doctors and therapist—no offense to any of those. Just the daily reminder.

I was assigned new therapists this week and they are definitely not as efficient. That's ok, but it sure was nice to get in and out of Vandy and be rolling back into Bowling Green by 10:15. Radiation is par for the course I suppose. I have a little rash going on and the chest pain started last week and is gradually building. I'd say my esophagus is somewhere between "rare" and "medium rare" on the cooked scale. Just a funny sensation in there.

But I will take that over chemo anytime. I learned early on I better get comfortable with being uncomfortable and at least attempt to look at anything related to pain as only a temporary physical sensation and not attach all the other stuff to it that can make it a lot worse. That's helped.

On Monday we had our annual Labor Day canoe trip. Conditions were great and we had a nice crowd. It was nice to reach the 3rd stop on my vision board. One more to go.

The 4th and final stop on my vision board is Watercolor, Florida for Fall Break which is coming in the first week of October. Unfortunately my final scan looks like it will be after that since radiation was pushed back. I was hoping to be all done and have that final scan in and clean and in the books before heading south. Oh well. Just the way it goes.

So there's this woman at radiation who is a little bit nutty. Ok more than a little bit. She is very loud and constantly talking to everyone who walks by. Which is fine. She gets wheeled around by her very patient caregiver. She laughs and swears a lot. Did I mention she is loud? And swears a lot? She provides a little entertainment and lightens the mood for the rest of us which is helpful. I usually only hear her because I am usually in and out so quick.

But not today. I was in the waiting room for a good forty-five minutes and got to spend a little time with her. She's probably 70-ish and hair is patchy and she's frail in body but underneath she has a lot of spirit. My guess is she's not long for this world, unfortunately. She could swear that I was someone famous. She just knew I was someone famous. I was wearing my Olympic Team USA shirt and she just knew I was in the Olympics.

So I leaned in and whispered and told her I was actually Michael Phelps but not to tell anyone. Which she promptly announced to everyone in the waiting room and anyone who walked by that Michael Phelps is here.

So we had this ongoing charade about the Olympics and my legal "misunderstandings." Strictly medicinal purposes of course, I explained. We talked about my training for Rio and why retirement didnt work for me.

She got called before me and as the therapist came to get her she said in her very loud voice "Holy !#&%, did you know that's Michael Phelps!" She winked at me as she wheeled by. I winked back and said a little prayer for her. And her caregiver.

As I was leaving this morning a lot of the therapist made a point to say goodbye to me and called me Michael.

Done
By Dan Klein — September 5, 2014

We have finally arrived at the finish line of treatment. Thank you Lord. Claire joined me on Monday and it was nice to have my cute girl with me. No marching bands or fireworks as we walked out of Vanderbilt's Ingram Cancer Center. Just another quiet victory on this journey. I've always appreciated quiet victories. None more than this one.

It's a good feeling having chemo and radiation behind me. It's slowly starting to sink in. It's been a long haul. A very long haul. As we had our ice cream and did our devotion the day's title said it all: "Weak and Weary." It reminded me that the January 13th title when all this nonsene began was "Expect Surprises."

I don't know how God does that but somehow there's always something around that reminds me He is there and taking care of me. It's just a matter if I choose to see it.

Back to work this week fulltime. Sort of. Jodi had a very nice reception for me for my first official day back. Thank you Jodi and to all my coworkers and clients who stopped by. That's a nice way to come back.

My after-treatment scan is scheduled for November 12th. Between now and then I am getting my port out. It will be nice to get the little sucker out of there. It's been an uneasy truce. I know what it's there for but it's still a bit of a pain to have that in there. Looking forward to getting that out but not so much to getting my 5th and, hopefully, final scar. Another little line of the story written on my chest.

I also need to do some other tests to figure out why some of my blood levels are quirky. I'm not looking forward to those. But it ain't chemo. And if it ain't chemo I can do it. I need to schedule that, but am enjoying not having to be the patient. But David is staying on my case to get it scheduled.

So if the November scan is clean then we begin the next leg of the journey which is getting to the one year mark— July 2015—then "Remission"—July 2016—and then being officially given the "Cure" title—July 2019. That's a long way off and there are a lot of scans between here and there. Plenty of opportunities for moments of anxiety and corresponding prayer.

I'll do my best not to dwell on the "what ifs" but I dont think I'd be human if I didn't. So I'll allow them to come out now and then when something stirs them and then send them back.

From here Claire and I slip into this invisible society of people somewhere on the range of patient/caregiver to survivors. We all walk past them and work with them and cut them off on the road every day. I experienced the last one a lot driving back and forth to Nashville: "Don't worry about me friend. I'm sure you got something more important to do than me. I'm just going to, you know, cancer treatment."

You just never know what someone is going through.

Returning to Normal Routine
By Claire Klein — November 5, 2014

It has really been nice to return to our "normal" life. Although, I have to say that Dan was always hanging tough. We were able to spend our Fall Break in WaterColor, FL with my parents and our friends, the Yerics. The weather was perfect and fun times were had by all. Life is so precious!

How could we have been there a year ago and have not an inkling of what the year ahead would hold? Growing up, I always wished that we could freeze times like these when we are all healthy and together.

These two months have flown by. We continue to be thankful for our family and friends. All Dan's prayer group fellows and accountability buds.

We also added a new member to our family, Rosebud. When Natalie asked her devoted daddy for a puppy last year, he told her she could get one for her birthday. She did NOT forget, and is happily turning five next week with a new pup.

Which brings us to next week...Nov. 12 is Dan's first scan post radiation. So, with a little trepidation, we will travel back to Vandy, to spend our day getting labs, a PET, and a visit to David and Leslie. Calling all Prayer Warriors... continue or get back on your knees, please!!

Note from Claire

Moving on...After six months of biweekly chemo treatments, seventeen daily radiation treatments, and a 5,200 mile minivan trip with the six of us out west in July of '15, we have moved on with our norm. With trepidation, we travel back down to Vandy every three months for checkups, praying for that Good News and hoping to get to that two year mark called remission and five years marked cured. If there was any luck involved, we realize that we were lucky to be dealt Hodgkin's lymphoma and not an illness with worse outcomes.

Recently, I nonchalantly asked the boys if they still worry about their Dad having had cancer. Matthew, who has a very joyful spirit about him stated, "not really." Ben, who is more sensitive, replied that yes he worries but it is not a big worry. John, the oldest and wisest, said he still thinks about it a lot. He says he has flashbacks of his dad having cancer. In fifth grade, when Dan was diagnosed, it seems to be most real to him. Once a year at mass, they have a beautiful ceremony with Anointing of the Sick. Anyone who has an illness, a significant past illness, preparing for surgery, pregnancy or something that one feels they need a blessing, that person stands. A priest comes to that person while everyone sitting close surrounds that person and lays their hands on them. The priest blesses the person with special oil that has been blessed by the bishop on Holy Thurs day and prays a special blessing. It is a very powerful moment. Many of us are moved to tears by this beautiful sacrament. Unbeknownst to me, John told me that this is a very emotional moment for him. He said that it makes him cry every time.

One day, a few months after Dan's treatments were final, Matthew said two good things came out of his dad having cancer. #1: Dad didn't lose all of his hair. #2: People became more catholic. How awesome that he picked up on this? And out of everything that Dan went through, he is most touched by the truth in this last statement. Friends and family couldn't help but be drawn into Dan's spiritual life by reading his entries. People became witnesses of his faith and grew stronger in their faith. Through this experience, we have become stronger, more aware, more focused, and more giving.

I have been blessed with this wonderful man as my soulmate. When others start saying nice things about Dan, I let them know, "what you see is what you get." He is truly an exceptional person. Cancer has given him a new lease on life, and he is living it to the fullest. He strives to be the best man that he can be. Those of us in his circle are fortunate to benefit from his zeal. Dan brings people together. We are spending more time gathered as families whether it be playing wiffleball or kickball in the yard followed by s'mores or canoeing down the Green River. He has made us all more service oriented. We find ourselves spending a couple of Sundays in the fall with families raking yards for elderly parishioners at our church. Dan lines up a group of fathers and children to chop and stack wood for an elderly lady who has a wood burning stove. At Christmas time, families caravan to a Christmas tree farm to pick up the trees for our church. Our friends are often laughing wondering what Dan will have us volunteered for next.

We all realize the good that comes from these acts of service. Sometimes, we just need that extra nudge. And Dan will not hesitate to give it.

Nobody gets a guarantees in life. We are living in the moment attempting to make the most of each day. We have grown in our faith, we love stronger, we try to be of service to those in need, and we try to appreciate what we have. Life has returned to normal. And with no delays or surprises, the six of us are preparing to hop in my minivan and head back out west again.

Clean Scan!
By Dan Klein — November 12, 2014

The official report will come out later this week but both the radiologist oncologist and our main doctor said it looked great. Thanks for all the prayers, support, and check ins today.

I'm sure one of us will post later with a little more detail but wanted to get the word out and say thanks to everyone.

Closing this chapter in our lives
By Dan Klein — December 12, 2014

So this is my fourth run at writing this. I must say after making thirty-five or so visits to Vanderbilt over an eigth month period it's been really nice to not go there and forget all about this whole cancer thing. And I think CaringBridge, as wonderful and as much of a blessing and convenient communication tool that it is, probably falls into the same mental category. It draws me back into the world of cancer and if you don't have to go there why the heck would you? But it's time.

So sorry for the delay but I appreciate the understanding. The official results were clean as expected. No big surprise there. Almost an afterthought based on what the doctors told us. But it is nice to get the official nod.

So from here we go back in February for a routine follow up visit and then a few months later for the next scan. And I imagine we will repeat that cycle for several years. I must say it was a little different for me going back to

Vandy in November. I think I was more aware of other people this time. That was a little depressing. I guess it's easier to think about one cancer story than dozens and dozens.

I also heard more. I was more aware of other people's conversations and got little glimpses into their world. When I would go for chemo I would just focus on getting prepared for taking care of what I needed to make it through that round and pretty much blocked everything else out.

Don't miss that chemo nonsense. As a general rule anything that makes your hair either fall out, turn different colors and/or textures, or changes the direction the darn stuff grows is not good for you. For the record I did not get the orange afro as I requested.

I will also say it's been much more of a mental game since treatment ended than I expected. That took some work and will probably continue to evolve. I'm sure some people who go through something like cancer struggle with the mental game for a long time if not forever. And why wouldn't you? Who knows better than someone who has gone through it that it could come again and life changes on some random Monday morning between dropping your kids off to school and going to work. One phone call. One trip to the doctor. One stinking cough.

This may seem obvious but until I went through treatments this fact just never dawned on me. Life during treatments is a horrible way to live. Ignorance can be an ally in that respect. I'd say that was very helpful the first couple of rounds. Not having any idea of what hell was about to be unleashed was a good thing. But now knowing one day you feel just fine and in a week or two you can be back in chemo plugged in and the poison dripping again is a terrible awareness.

And if that does happen then you spend the next so many months or maybe even the rest of your life feeling horrible. That's no way to live. And having the understanding and knowing with absolute certainty that it is indeed just one phone call away is a tough one to cozy up to.

And what really ratchets up the difficult level is every day getting these little cancer reminders. Chemo has seemingly an endless number of potential side effects. Some short term and some long term. They serve as constant reminders of cancer. So just like getting alerts on my phone I get pinged by cancer.

The side effects that I am walking away with could be a lot worse and I'm thankful for that. I can live with them. Hopefully they get better and go away but they may not. And that's ok. I've just mentally locked down and accepted that they're here to stay. And if they get better that's a bonus. But they are always there. Every day.

So after radiation wrapped up in September I didn't really get the rush of excitement of being done with cancer. Yes, great to finish treatments and turn that page. But I'm going through this mental obstacle course of awaiting my November scan and all the fun that you can imagine comes with that. Then thinking about doing this whole scan thing every few months for the next several years and hoping and praying you don't get launched back into chemo and the world that is cancer. And at the same time getting pinged a couple of dozen times a day with cancer reminders to bring all that to the front of your mind all day long.

I'm praying about it and trying to sort it out. Wondering if this weird and crappy place of worrying if cancer will come back and getting dumped back into chemo is where I'm going to have to hang out for the next few months? Few years? Rest of my life?

I'm not warming up to this one so easily here, dear Lord. Help me out. So between a lot of conversations with God, some wisdom from silence, and finally reaching out to my special friend and fellow cancer survivor Leslie and having her perspective it all came together.

Whatever comes down the pipe I will be able to handle. God has either already equipped me with the tools— whether I'm aware of them or not—or will make them available to me to get through whatever comes. A lot of those tools being people—you. People who have been in my life for a long time or who have come into my life through this experience. The prayers, meals, visits, drop offs, cards—all those things that may not seem so sig- nificant in and of themselves but on the whole become this gigantic incredible work of compassion. There are no words for that. They simply don't exist.

Having that confidence is a pretty liberating feeling. It's almost an unfair advantage in life to have that perspec- tive. Having the peace and confidence of not worrying about what could happen down the road. Just being able to enjoy today. Thanking God on credit—not sure how you're going to get us through this one but thanks for whatever solution you're going to provide because I know it will be there. That's the gift of cancer.

That has made me aware of the words of a sentence I've breezed through probably a million times—"Give us this day our daily bread."

Give me what I need for today. Whatever I have to face I'll have the tools and weapons and, most importantly, the people around me I need to meet those challenges. I'll have my daily bread today and tomorrow will take care of itself. And help me to make myself willing and available to be that for others.

And rather than see these daily pings as negative reminders of the beast that is cancer and can be again, I choose to see them as my daily reminders of what a wonderful life I have. Having the memory of getting unplugged from the IV, standing up slowly, and strapping on my backpack to walk slowly down the chemo hallway with that headache already setting in is a powerful reminder of how precious life is and how quickly the things I can so easily take for granted—eating, sleeping, being able to get out of bed, feeling human—can be snatched away.

There are still tough days and struggles and stresses that come along with normal life on top of emerging from life with cancer. But I recognize how blessed I am to have an incredible wife and healthy kids to love and who love me. A warm home and food in the fridge when I open it. A great extended family and circle of friends to experience life with that allows us to divide our struggles and multiply our joys. My catholic faith, the faith community of Holy Spirit, and a close and personal relationship with a loving and compassionate God. And the understanding of how wonderful today really is when I treat it as it is so appropriately named—the present.

Merry Christmas everyone. Enjoy your present.

Reflections From the End of the Dock: 90-Day Checkout

L iving life on a 90-day checkout from the cancer center can
be tough. It can make for relentless mental and emotional
torment. Or it can be a gift. It's a matter of how you choose to
approach it. I try not to think and worry about it too much—at
least until we get close to the appointment. From there, I do my
best to use the gift of perspective that cancer has provided me
to handle it the best I can.

I believe the way you approach a cancer check-up is no
different than the way you approach any challenge in life. We
all have cancers of some manner, shape, or size. Yes, they can be
abnormal cells that take the form of a tumor in your chest. Or
they can be personal or professional challenges that can wreak

havoc on us emotionally, psychologically, and ultimately physically. A broken relationship. A difficult professional or financial situation. A void of spiritual connectedness and fullness. A feeling of anxiety about the future, or not having any clue or sense of purpose of where or what that future is.

As I worked through that process of trying to move on from that always present threat of cancer I finally came to the realization that I had a choice. Every day I had a choice. Every single day, consciously or not, I made the choice to carry with me or leave behind certain things. On the road out of cancer and back to life at some point I stopped and put down my mental and emotional backpack. I began to sift through all the stuff that accumulated in there. I allowed myself to keep certain things to bring forward in my life and chose to leave other things on the side of the road.

I can take with me a deeper understanding of my faith and my relationship with God. The gifts of family and friends who, when I needed them the most, stepped up to the plate and absolutely nailed it. The perfect understanding that every day is a new day and all I have to do is focus on one day at a time and do the absolute best I can with it. And when things aren't going my way it's ok to pause, reflect, and restart or redirect. And my prize possession, the one essential to living in a state of grace, is the understanding that my energy is focused only on those things within my control. I can't do anymore than that.

I can leave behind all that anxiety, fear, and concern. I can leave behind all those thoughts of missing out on the kids growing up or growing old with Claire. I can leave behind the burden of awareness that someday cancer can come back and I will die a long, slow, and painful death. All the energy and worry in the world won't do a darn thing to change any of those. Why in the world would I give those things power over me? The only one that allows me to carry that stuff forward is me.

And the real crappy thing about not dumping that stuff on the side of the road is not only am I shouldering that unnecessary burden but I have to focus on that garbage that I have zero control over and, here's the kicker, it prevents me from enjoying and experiencing the very life that those things make me so afraid to lose.

Every day I can make that choice of what I'm bringing forward with me and what I'm leaving behind. When I'm at my best, I take just the good stuff. I'm light on my feet. Just packing the carry-on with me on the airplane of life. Not checking that darn oversized suitcase of crap. There most certainly are days when, for whatever reason, I set down my carry-on and I pick up that bulky baggage. I feel the burden and its weight until I realize what I'm doing and the gift of cancer reminds me to put that thing down. I don't have to carry that.

I, like most, am a creature of habit. When I'm in the routine and doing all those life push-ups I sail through life in a state of grace. I move with purpose because I know where I'm going. I know where the end of the dock is and I know all I have to do, all I can do, is focus on just today and focus on just the things within my control to move me one step closer.

First Song Out of One Year Check Up
By Dan Klein — October 24, 2015

"Fight Song" by Rachel Platten

This is my fight song. Take back my life song.
Prove I'm alright song. My powers turned on.
Starting right now I'll be strong. I'll play my fight song.
And I don't really care if nobody else believes
Cause I still got a lot of fight left in me!

Everything is great. Clean visit. Hard to believe it's been one year since the final radiation treatment. The goal is to be clean two years from the last treatment date. That would be September 8, 2016. A date circled on my calendar.

Hodgkins lymphoma has between an eight and ten percent chance of something coming back within the first two years. One year down and one year to go. "Cured" is five years. Ahh, that's a long time. We will continue to go back every three-to-four months for check-ups. I do my best not to worry about it. Easier said than done sometimes. But I know better than anyone worrying about something you have little or no control over is useless.

When I get about a week or so from our check-up date it starts popping in my head a little more often.

Knowing you are one bad visit away from being launched back into chemo and the fight is not a pleasant thought. That's ok. I allow it to come out and do its thing and then move on. Going through life on a ninety day checkout from the cancer center presents some minor challenges but it's a gift. I'm thankful to have this gift of awareness and perspective and the strong refresher course every ninety days. It's a pretty easy reset button to be reminded that I don't have problems.

We continue to love and laugh. To do our devotion and, of course, eat ice cream. A little more than before for all of the above. My mornings still begin with a candle, coffee, and morning prayer. Rather than reading Proverbs I now read the gospels one chapter at a time. My time spent in Proverbs leading up to and through cancer I now see as preparation and training. Thank you Lord for that gift. It seems fitting now to spend my time in the gospels following the daily walk of Jesus.

It's been a busy year when we look back on it. I can't say we really set out to do a bunch of things. I suppose we were just open to them. Instead of immediately thinking of all the reasons we shouldn't do something we just think "why not."

We finally pulled the trigger on remodeling our home that we had been kicking around for the last several years. Claire and I recognize we have a special ten years coming at us. A chapter in our lives where we have our family under one roof before the kids slowly begin their march towards independence.

We also had a new addition to the family. When you are going through cancer and your five year old daughter looks at you and says "Daddy, can I have a puppy?" there's only one answer. RoseBud joined us last September. I survived cancer but living through a remodel and a puppy at the same time was often in doubt.

After fifteen years with my employer we parted ways. I started my own firm and purposefully named it Lockshield Partners. A nod to making sure you have the right people —the right partners—around you. That's critical in life— be it professional or personal. Partners to lock shields with to make you stronger when you need them and to make them stronger when they need you. Sometimes complacency is not your friend but a convenient companion.

I got together with my college buddies in Jackson Hole, Wyoming in February. Almost a year to the day that they surprised me and spent the weekend with me. Old friends are special friends.

Every other Wednesday at 6:00 AM I get to eat breakfast with a phenomenal group of men who I have the privilege to call friends. We pray and laugh and share with each other our successes and struggles and do our best to become better husbands, fathers, friends, and followers of the teachings of Jesus Christ.Thanks guys for being there with us every step of the way.

We finally got to make our trip out West. We had planned our great adventure before this whole cancer nonsense. A good old fashion Griswold vacation road trip. We were hitting the road and going out west to the national parks and wherever the winds took us. Maps were laid out on the kitchen table with potential routes highlighted. We watched Youtube videos of buffalo maulings and bear attacks as I gently reassured the kids: Remember you don't have to be the fastest you just can't be the slowest.

But all that got set aside when cancer invaded our home. So it was that much more meaningful this year as we planned and prepared to finally make our trip. Maps with potential routes highlighted once again laid out on the kitchen table and YouTube videos once again became part of our nightly devotions. We pulled out of the driveway on July 5th. The day after Independence Day. That was not lost on me. What a cool thing to be able to do to just pile in the van and go wherever you want to go. We spent the better part of three weeks traveling and covered 5,200 miles. I'd do it again tomorrow.

It's funny a lot of people have made the comment to us how much they have always wanted to do that kind of trip. I typically don't give unsolicited advice so rather than smacking them in the head and saying "Don't wait! Do it now you big dummy!" I just say something along the lines of, "There's no time like the present." There's never a better time than right now to do what you always wanted to do.

Three days after we returned from that marathon of a trip Matthew and I headed to the Great Northern Woods for the annual Hartman gathering at BHL. Great to see the family and pay my visit to the end of the dock. A visit I hope to make many, many more times. A highlight of my year would by making a surprise twenty-four hour round trip to Ann Arbor, Michigan. Dad's cancer had returned and he was quickly scheduled for surgery. A surgery that would prove to be successful. I knew what it meant to get unexpected support. So I drove the 500+ miles to AA and arrived around 10:00 that night. I knocked on their hotel room door and Dad opened the door. The surprise look on his face and the hug that ensued was something I will always remember. It was great to spend an hour or so with Mom & Dad that night and to have breakfast and pray with them the next morning before Dad headed to surgery and I headed back to Kentucky. It was nice to be on the giving end rather than the receiving end for a change. I know who gets the most out of that.

I'm not sure if I fully realized or appreciated what my mom has experienced the last few years. It's bad enough to have your spouse go through cancer. And it's bad enough to have your child go through cancer. But to go through both of those at the same time is a heavy cross to bear. I remember growing up whenever something bad would happen to us my Mom would say "I'm sorry." That confused me because whatever it was certainly wasn't her fault. So finally one time I said "You didn't do anything. What are you sorry for?" And she calmly replied "I'm not sorry that I did anything. I'm just sorry you have to experience it."

I'm sorry Mom.

The next time I saw Dad was when I made an eventful trip to 1,000 miles north of Nowhere,Manitoba to join him and my brothers for a fishing trip. Two nights before I was set to depart for this much anticipated trip Claire figured out that, yes,I did indeed need a passport to get to Canada and, no, it can't be expired. Details! After calling the airlines and trying desperately to find a way to get a passport or an exception somehow from someone I was told I was absolutely not going to cross the border.

That wasn't an option. I tried everything including calling my congressman (thank you Brett Guthrie's office!). I altered my flights and left the house at 2:30AM with a slight chance of making it across the border. I spent the better part of the day in the US State Department office in Minneapolis. Thirty minutes before their office closed for the weekend they called my name. I got that darn passport and breathed a sigh of relief as I finally stepped from the gangway on to the plane for the 11:30 PM flight from Minneapolis to Winnipeg that night. A day late but I made it to fish camp. The four of us having plenty of laughs, sharing every meal together, playing cards, encountering a 3 legged black bear,and sleeping in the same room in our little cabin. Where's there's a will there's a way. Fish on!

I physically feel great. The minor side effects that I left treatment with haven't gotten much better but that's ok. I can deal with them. I have what I have come to refer to as "My 3:59." That's my nod to Roger Bannister who was the first runner to break the four minute mile. To do something once thought impossible. What your mind tells your body matters and I know that regardless if I think I can or think I can't I'm probably right.

And I have started writing. Some days it's nice to leave all that cancer BS behind me and look forward and never look back. But I have gained from my experience. I recognize others have as well. It may not ever sit on a bookshelf other than my own but I feel called to share my journey in hopes that others may benefit without paying the toll that cancer collects.

I've come to view life as this metaphorical ride. Complete with ups and downs and twist and turns. Surrounded by family and friends we experience this ride together. Then one day the monster that is cancer shows up out of the blue. It stops the ride—because it can—and points at you and motions for you to step off the ride. That's a tough one to swallow. But it doesn't compare to watching that ride slowly start to move away from you with everyone that means anything to you still onboard going on while you do your best to smile and wave goodbye.

That's the hardest part. You can imagine the appreciation when you get a chance to get back on that ride. You look at the ups and downs, the twists and turns, and especially the people around you differently. You recognize each part of the ride has its own unique qualities—good and bad—and you appreciate it all. You can't help but sneak a peak around the corner every now and then knowing cancer or something else can be waiting for you. Or someone next to you.

And you recognize that the ride will indeed someday come to an end for all of us. Sooner or later we will all get asked to step off the ride. At that moment we will either be full of contentment and appreciation for what we had or regret and sorrow for what we didn't do. And at that point there's not a damn thing you can do about it.

I resolve to spend my days from this one to that one to be able to genuinely smile and wave goodbye with a heart full of contentment and appreciation knowing I lived a life worth living. I ran my race. I finished strong. I did the best I could with the gifts God gave me. And I look forward to standing in front of God and asking forgiveness for where I fell short and giving an account for the time He granted me.

Thank you again to everyone for your tremendous support, prayers, and acts of love. We're all capable of those and there is no shortage of need. I'm glad to be back on the giving side of the equation with you. You never know how that card, prayer, visit, text, or email touches someone. Somehow they always seem to land at just the right the moment. Keep giving. It's often the smallest of gestures that ripple through time and space that mean so much. The butterfly effect.

Like a small boat on the ocean
sending big waves in motion.
Like how a single word
can make a heart open
I may only have one match
But I can cause an explosion.
Yes, indeed, I still got
a lot of fight left in me.

My 3:59

On a windy Friday on a track in Oxford, England Roger Bannister became the first person to run a mile in less than four minutes. The year was 1954. Prior to that it was just understood that the human body was not physically capable of doing it. But once Bannister broke the barrier, it took just forty-six days for another runner to achieve the impossible. Within a decade a high schooler from Kansas did it.

Roger Bannister, the runner would go on to become Dr. Roger Bannister the neurologist. Neurologist specialize in the nervous system which include the brain and the spinal cord. What the brain tells the body matters. What we believe to be possible—or impossible—is incredibly significant.

In 2013, pre-cancer, I set a goal to be able to dunk a basketball. It had been many years since I had been able to do that. I was turning forty and it seemed like a good stretch goal. My own little act of defiance against Father Time. I laid out my plans to achieve it and worked hard at it. I gave it real effort. But, in the end, my days of playing above the rim were over. I just couldn't do it. To be honest, not even close. I chalked it up that my time had passed and it wasn't possible. I turned forty and left dunking behind me.

Then, less than a year later, on that random Monday morning, cancer came calling. After experiencing all that cancer put me through, not only physically but probably more meaningful emotionally, psychologically, and spiritually I walked away with a different perspective. A very different perspective on what I can and can't do. What was possible and what was impossible.

I walk away from cancer with some minor side effects from treatment. Being a chemical dump for months on end carries with it a permanent price. My daily reminders of my time with the Rumble. I'd rather not have them but I can deal with them. Despite them, and my age, I have what I refer to as "My 3:59." My symbolic gesture of doing something once thought impossible.

After getting my clean PET scan in November of 2014 I set that goal to dunk again. I reached out to a friend who was a personal trainer and told her what I wanted to do. I also brought in Claire, of course, and my accountability buddies and made them aware of what I was trying to achieve. Now it wasn't just a goal in my head. Someone else not only knew about it but had the expertise to help me accomplish it and I had accountability to people who mattered. I placed that stake in the ground. No, I pounded that stake in the ground.

I worked hard. I leaned in. I wasn't going to just plug my way through a work out. I wasn't going to just go through the motions. Griping about it the whole time just to check it off my list. This was about more than dunking a basketball. I was reclaiming my life. Just six months before I struggled to get my right foot to the floor to start the long and difficult process of just getting out of bed. I am all in. I am going for this. I am owning it. It will happen.

There would be spurts of progress and times of stubborn resistance. By mid-April I had come a long way but was still short an inch or two. So I called an old friend who works at Western Kentucky University and asked if he could get me on the floor. I told him I wanted to take a pass from Big Red, the loveable WKU mascot, on the hardwood of Diddle Arena and to do my impossible.

Donald was very gracious and said to just let him know when I wanted to get into the arena and he would make it happen. He offered to get a bunch of students as a cheering section holding signs to make for a good photo or video shot. Thanks, but not necessary. This one's for me. I just need my family and a couple of close friends.

I told Claire I was close and called those friends and asked if they would be willing to come. We set the date for two weeks. I had two short weeks to get over that stubborn hump.

It took me almost six months of training but four days after my 42nd birthday and, much more meaningful, ten months after the last drop of chemotherapy was pumped into my veins, we pulled up to the empty parking lot of Diddle Arena. We met Donald and walked onto that large court in an empty arena.

We shot around and played a little bit to get loose. And then I went for it. It took several attempts. Enough where I think everyone in the gym was beginning to wonder. I could feel my thigh muscles starting to talk to me. My fingers were starting to bleed a little from my failed attempts. But then it happened. I took the bounce pass from Big Red as I crossed the free throw line cutting through the lane, made one dribble, and attacked the rim and flushed it. I got my dunk. I achieved my 3:59.

It was a little microcosm for life. Lay out the worthy and meaningful goals. Give more than you think you have to achieve them. Have your family and a few really good friends around you to support you and to experience it together. What else is there?

Pretty cool way to go through life when you stop thinking about all the reasons you can't do something and just de-

---

[1] If you got a minute pull it up and make sure you read the rest of the story. You can go to Youtube and search "my 3:59 Dan Klein"

cide not only you can but you will. The really cool thing about a 3:59 is you come to this realization that the only limitations you have are largely self-imposed. If I can dunk a basketball at forty-two, just ten months after finishing chemo, what can't I do??

With that perspective I set out for my next 3:59. The BG26.2. That's a marathon in Bowling Green. I'm not a runner. I ran a 5k years ago and hated every step of it. But I can walk. I got legs that work so I figured I might as well use them. Often we don't fully appreciate things—or people—until they are taken away from us.

I know what it's like for your body to be broken. I know what it's like to curl up in a bed in the cancer center and hurt. I know what it's like for your wife to softly kiss your forehead after she puts a heated blanket over you to ward off the shakes. I know what it's like to do a big exhale and watch as the IV drip starts and the poison begins to flow yet again. And I know what it's like to have to fight to just get out of bed.

I've paid too much to take life for granted.

I don't see a marathon as 26.2 miles. That's too much. Just like it's too much to do two hundred and seventeen days of cancer treatment. I'm not capable of that. But I can do one mile twenty-six times. I can manage one day of cancer treatment two hundred and seventeen times. Some will be easier than others. I recognize that. And I recognize at the starting line there are no guarantees of ever seeing the finish line. But I still line up. Ready to go.

I gave thought and identified my goal. I put in the work, I trained, and I completed my marathon. I notched my next "My 3:59." The kids met me at the final turn and escorted me the final hundred yards. Claire was standing at the finish line with my medal, her cute smile, and a great big hug.

What your mind tells your body indeed matters. And regardless if you think you can or think you can't you're probably right. And who and what you have around you matters.

As it so often happens in life, my marathon included a detour. A deviation from the well planned out route. Somewhere around mile twenty-four the course went past the hospital—the very hospital where we experienced not only the birth of our children but the initial cancer scans and biopsies as well. The same place where people at that very moment were not only taking chemo and radiation, but experiencing who knows what other kind of pain and suffering.

At the corner where the hospital complex ends the marathon course, well marked, turned to the left. I, on the other hand, turned to the right. Within a minute a race official had caught up with me to tell me I was off course. I smiled and assured him I was not and I would be back.

I made the almost mile long loop around the hospital before getting back on course. Legs tired. Spirit strong. I prayed. I thanked God for my healing and for being on the outside of the hospital. I prayed for the patients inside, for their healing, and that they would know God's peace and grace as He allowed me to.

I knew they laid just beyond the windows that I could so easily see. So many windows. Six floors of them. So many patients. So much suffering. How often I looked out of my window at Vanderbilt, IV dripping, at the passing cars and people casually walking about their busy lives. How I wished to be anywhere but right there in that room. How I longed for the day to be back in the world of the healthy and capable. And here I am. Good and gracious Lord, here I am.

Afterword: Letter to My Kids

Dear John, Matthew, Ben, & Natalie,

When I finally got the treatment stage of cancer behind me and began to navigate the process of going back to the cancer center every 3-4 months for check-ups I couldn't help but feel a sense of urgency to teach you everything a Dad is supposed to. The awareness of how precious yet how fleeting time was made me want to compress a lifetime of fathering into a condensed and forced version.

But I discovered, very quickly, somethings aren't meant to be rushed. Certain lessons in life unfold according to their own natural order and sequence of experiences. Some lessons are easy and straight forward. Others require patience and consistency and finally take root all of a sudden over a long period of time.

I also humbly accepted that I don't have all the answers. Nor do I even know all the right questions. Some things I know for sure. But others I am still figuring out on my own. We're supposed to have all the answers and always do the right thing. Yet, not a day goes by that I don't make mistakes. There's a certain level of pretense or perhaps even hypocrisy in being a parent. For it is impossible for me to teach you what I have yet to master. I can't give to you what I don't fully own. I think being a parent and a Christian are similar in that regard.

But with that awareness I learned a valuable lesson. A critical piece to the puzzle that is life. Kids, nobody ever figures it all out. We are all a constant work in progress. In this life there is no one end destination. You never fully arrive. We are a continual series of destinations along our own path. Your life's work is to make sure you are on the right path and in times, for whatever reason, when you wander from it to find your way back.

In school you will learn about our country's founding fathers. Names like Washington, Jefferson, and Franklin. They had the foresight to know that in putting into writing the basis and foundation for our country's freedoms, rights, and obligations there was no way they could address all current and future situations. So they wisely laid a foundation through the Constitution based on timeless principles.

So, too, I have found certain timeless principles when it comes to life. What you stand for. What you believe in. How to find your path. To move with purpose towards the next destination and to be able to overcome obstacles along the way.

I hope and pray to have the natural life span of a father to watch you grow through all the various stages of your life's journey. To love and encourage you. To guide you and pick you up and brush you off when you stumble. To be able to pass on these timeless principles to you in the natural order of time. In doing so hopefully they will allow you to live a fulfilling and meaningful life of peace and grace and, in turn, pass them on to your children and beyond.

But in the event I don't have that natural life span I need you to know those principles. I need you to have that foundation for your own personal constitution. The framework through which you can approach all of life's ups and downs. Four specific cornerstones to build a life worth living.

First of all, at the basis of everything, is effort. Be it your education, your professional life or—more meaningful—your personal relationships and spiritual life. There is absolutely no substitute for hard work. Just bring it! Whatever you are doing give it all you got. You have more than you think to give. You are able to do more than your mind and body will lead you to believe. Don't settle for anything in this life. Don't just go through the motions of a job or of a marriage or of being a parent or friend and certainly don't just go through the motions of your spiritual life. Too many people do that and then wonder why they don't get anything out of it. Whatever you do, put everything into it. See discipline as your partner not your adversary and don't accept the good when the great is just one more level of effort away. Constantly push.

I love the look on Roger Bannister's face as he crosses the finish line for his first 3:59. It is a look of giving absolutely everything. In that same photo you will notice all the people standing and watching on the inside of the track. You will see that in your own life. Most people will opt to stand idly by and are content to watch life go by them rather than taking the risk and putting forth the effort to get on the track. Step on that track kids. When you run your various races of life and pour everything you have into them it will make your successes and achievements that much more meaningful. And even in times where you fall short, and certainly you will, you will live without regret knowing you gave it your all. Knowing you lived life on the track.

Second is the butterfly effect. Just as a butterfly that flaps its wings in South America can alter the course of a tornado in Texas so too will your actions ripple through time and space. You will never know the extent—good or bad—the actions you do—or don't do—will have on your life as well as on the lives of others. You may from time to time have the opportunity to do big things with large impacts. But recognize the vast majority of your life will be an accumulation of the many small daily actions you decide to take. Set your sights on what is important. Wake up every day and go to work every day doing the little things that in the aggregate lead you along your path from destination to destination.

Third, and most difficult, is resolve. Despite the effort and the countless daily actions you will get knocked down. Just accept that failure is part of the human experience. Anything worth having in this life requires real effort and risk. Otherwise it wouldn't be worth having. Otherwise everyone would already have it. Know when you begin you will be tested and questioned. In life sometimes you have to go through Good Friday to get to Easter Sunday.

You have two powerful allies at your disposal in resolve —the grace of the Holy Spirit and the awareness of today. When something is beyond you then seek God's grace through the Holy Spirit. It's so much easier than trying to do it all by yourself. There is nothing greater than the Holy Spirit. It's like having a super hero at your disposal. Learn in the stillness of silence to be able to harness the power of the Holy Spirit.

And when something gets so difficult that you feel so overwhelmed then just focus on today. Whatever "it" is don't think of it as something you have to deal with forever. The smallest obstacle can be insurmountable in that context. All you have to do is focus on is giving everything you got and getting through it today. Know what you are moving towards is worth the effort. Just keep moving. Put forth the effort. Do the little things every day that inch you closer and closer. And don't ever give up on something or someone you believe in.

Fourth, and most important, is finding your answer to the spiritual meaning of life. Find your path. Stay on your path. Make your way back when life steers you off course.

I'm no historian and no expert on spirituality. Just a reluctant author with no qualified training other than my own life's experiences. Just incredibly blessed to be given the greatest gifts I could receive in this world—to love your mother and to be your dad. But it occurred to me going through cancer that there are common threads throughout history that seem to transcend time, place, and religion. Maybe not perfect parallels. But enough tendencies to at least make me pause and take notice.

Looking back through history at many of the great thinkers and minds of the current and long ago cultures, the consistencies in their answers to the meaning of life is the presence of a higher spiritual power. If you lay out the beliefs and philosophies of those various civilizations next to each other you will start to see some remarkable resemblances. Just like your own constitution, timeless principles that regardless of geography, time, or religion seem to weave their way through the quest for the meaning of life and the question of is there really a God.

It seems those common threads existed in those very different cultures in those very different places in those very different times because they work. They make sense. They make us happy and bring us peace. Maybe at our core, embedded in our human DNA, some things have always been, are now, and always will be constant.

Thousands of years before the technology you use to share information instantly it was impossible for those different cultures to have much, if any, exposure to each other. Yet they all zeroed in on some of the same principles. Proverbs from King Solomon in Jerusalem almost 1,000 years BC. Taoism in China 600 years BC with the yin & yang and its own path. Socrates in Ancient Greece 400+ years BC with his ironic death sentence. The Great Spirit of many Native American nations. Ultimately, Jesus Christ himself, and our Catholic faith.

Know that Jesus Christ most certainly walked this very same earth that you and I do. Nobody denies that. And what he did 2,000 years ago was so amazing that billions of people today are still following his example and teachings. What are you and I going to ever do in this life that someone will even remember or take note of one hundred years after we're gone let alone 2,000 years? Yet there are people committing their entire lives to Him and His teachings to this day.

Your spiritual path will not always be smooth. It will not always be straight. But know that path is the right one to be on. Expect the curves and the peaks and the valleys. It's ok to question and to probe. It's ok to doubt. It's a natural sign of how incredible God is that we just can't wrap our human brains around that level of grace and awesomeness. God can handle that. For even the guys who walked daily with Jesus, the guys who witnessed the wedding at Canaan, who witnessed the blind see and the cripple walk, who saw with their own eyes Jesus walk on water, and who even saw Jesus die on the cross and then appeared to them after rising from the dead, had a hard time believing what they saw. Take comfort, as I do, that the guy who Jesus appointed as the cornerstone of His church on earth, the rock and foundation of the church, the first pope, denied him three times when Jesus needed him the most.

Did Jesus really turn water in wine? Did Jesus really make blind people see and the lame walk? Walk on water? And ultimately, the main question, did Jesus Christ really rise from the dead and walk out of that tomb? My answer to those questions, based on the gospels and my experiencing of His grace going through cancer, is a resounding yes. And with that answer than to the question of was Jesus the son of God, the divine made human to show us the way to live in this world so we could not only live forever in the next but live a life of meaning and grace while we're here, then my answer has to be absolutely.

I run the risk of oversimplifying my answer to the meaning of life. But then again, one of the gifts of cancer is you learn to do just that—simplify things. Maybe that is part of the answer. Maybe a bigger part than we all realize. When Jesus was asked about the most important commandments His reply was to first love the Lord your God with all your heart, all your soul, and all your mind. And, second, to love your neighbor as yourself.

There it is. Don't spend a lifetime looking for what has been placed right in front of you.

My hope and prayer is that you find the path that has been laid out for you and that you become the person God has called you to be.

I love you and I'm proud of you,

Dad

About the Author

Writer and speaker DAN KLEIN began the My3:59 movement with the dunk of a basketball. It was just after his 42nd birthday but much more meaningful than his age was it occurred seven months after his final cancer treatment.

"After going through everything cancer puts you through—physically, emotionally, psychologically, and spiritually—I came away with a different perspective on life. A very different perspective on what I can and what I can't do."

Going through cancer as a husband and father of four young children and facing the possibility of his life coming to an end, Dan made it his mission to live a life of approaching each day as it is so appropriately named: the present. Treating every day as a gift from God has allowed Dan to accomplish things he never dreamed he could do.

Since the dunk there have been marathons, starting his own business, finally taking the family on the long road trip out West, and learning to play the guitar. But the most significant impact of Dan's My3:59 approach to life is that he has inspired people around him to set their own 3:59's. And the 3:59 movement began.

Dan uses cancer as a proxy for any and all of the challenges we face in life. His message of determination, vision, and purpose resonates with a wide variety of people.

Dan is a sought-after keynote speaker and works with corporate leadership and sales teams. He has spoken at a wide variety of venues, ranging from national conferences, sales conferences, religious retreats, and even small country churches. Dan's message of living every day and giving everything you have to achieve your impossible in order to become the person we are called to be continues to inspire and motivate others to achieve their own My3:59.

To find out more about Dan or to schedule him as a speaker for your organization please visit the My3:59 Facebook page or www.mythreefiftynine.com